I0796555

# 美丽中国
# BEAUTIFUL CHINA

## 当代中国风景园林的思考
## Reflections on Landscape Architecture in Contemporary China

**ORO Editions**

Publishers of Architecture, Art, and Design
Gordon Goff: Publisher

www.oroeditions.com
info@oroeditions.com

Published by ORO Editions



Editor: Tatum L. Hands
Book Design: Chendi Zhang and Yifan Cai
Managing Editor: Jake Anderson

10 9 8 7 6 5 4 3 2 1 First Edition

ISBN: 978-1-943532-81-0

Color Separations and Printing: ORO Group Ltd.
Printed in China.

ORO Editions makes a continuous effort to minimize the overall carbon footprint of its publications. As part of this goal, ORO Editions, in association with Global ReLeaf, arranges to plant trees to replace those used in the manufacturing of the paper produced for its books. Global ReLeaf is an international campaign run by American Forests, one of the world's oldest nonprofit conservation organizations. Global ReLeaf is American Forests' education and action program that helps individuals, organizations, agencies, and corporations improve the local and global environment by planting and caring for trees.

# BEAUTIFUL CHINA

## Reflections on Landscape Architecture in Contemporary China

Richard J. Weller & Tatum L. Hands

ORO Editions
Los Angeles | San Francisco | New York | Shenzhen

## 美丽中国

“建设生态文明，关系人民福祉，关乎民族未来。中共十八大报告提出，努力建设美丽中国，实现中华民族永续发展。中共十九大报告进一步提出，加快生态文明体制改革，建设美丽中国。并且提出从2035年到本世纪中叶，在基本实现现代化的基础上，再奋斗十五年，把中国建成富强民主文明和谐美丽的社会主义现代化强国。建设美丽中国成为中国梦的重要内容。具体而言，就是要按照尊重自然、顺应自然、保护自然的原则，秉持“既要金山银山，又要绿水青山”“绿水青山就是金山银山”的理念，贯彻节约资源和保护环境的基本国策，更加自觉地推动绿色发展、循环发展、低碳发展；就是要给自然留下更多修复空间，给农业留下更多良田，为子孙后代留下天蓝、地绿、水清的生产生活环境。中国梦的实现不以牺牲环境为代价，在发展经济的同时，保护好生态环境。建设美丽中国，有利于中国的长远发展，也将助推世界可持续发展，更有助于实现人类共同的梦想——保护美丽的地球。”

国务院新闻办公室

## BEAUTIFUL CHINA

"A beautiful environment is beneficial to the people and the future of the nation. The report to the 18th National Congress of the Communist Party of China (CPC) called for hard work to build a beautiful country, and achieve lasting and sustainable development of the Chinese nation. The report to the 19th CPC National Congress proposed speeding up reform of the system for developing an ecological civilization, and building a beautiful China. It also set the goal of developing China into a great modern socialist country that is prosperous by the middle of the 21st century.

Building a beautiful China is an important part of the Chinese Dream. It calls for respecting, protecting and being in harmony with nature, based on the understanding that 'lucid waters and lush mountains are invaluable assets.' China should implement its key national policy on resource conservation, environmental protection, and promotion of green, circular and low-carbon development. The initiative underscores the need to leave more space for nature to renew itself, to keep more land for cultivation, and to bequeath a better working and living environment to future generations so that they can be blessed with blue sky, green fields, and clean water.

The Chinese Dream will not be realized at the expense of the environment. Economic development should be accompanied by strong measures to protect the environment. Building a beautiful China will be of benefit to the country's long-term development, to promoting sustainable global development, and to fulfilling the universal dream of protecting our beautiful earth."

**The State Council Information Office, The People's Republic of China**

# 目录 | CONTENTS

# 引言

# 前言
# Introduction

# Engaging with Beautiful China
# 参与美丽中国建设

**理查德·韦勒** | Richard WELLER

Professor and Chair of Landscape Architecture, Meyerson Chair of Urbanism, and Co-Executive Director of the McHarg Center, Stuart Weitzman School of Design, University of Pennsylvania.

宾夕法尼亚大学斯图尔特·威兹曼设计学院景观系主任，麦尔森城市化研究主席。

**塔特姆·汉兹** | Tatum HANDS

Editor in Chief, *LA+ Interdisciplinary Journal of Landscape Architecture*, and lecturer, Stuart Weitzman School of Design, University of Pennsylvania. Hands holds an honors degree in law and a PhD in political science and international relations.

宾夕法尼亚大学斯图尔特·威兹曼设计学院景观系讲师，LA+跨专业杂志主编。汉兹曾获得法律荣誉学位与政治科学与国际关系的博士学位。

In ancient Greece, the Pythagorean mystics (6th century BCE) believed that the quintessence of nature was mathematical and that this could be expressed in the form of geometric figures and music. Eulogized and assembled into a complete cosmology by Plato, these "forms" were considered signatures of the divine intelligence that created and transcends all things. This is what the Greeks of classical antiquity meant by beauty – or rather, *absolute* beauty.

Around the same time, though on the other side of the world, Chinese Taoists also sensed that nature contained a deep and unifying essence and found it profoundly beautiful. The Taoists believed that an appreciation of this beauty served as a guide for human nature. But whereas for the Greeks geometry was the key to its inner sanctum, for the Taoists beauty manifested in the wild landscape, in the mountains (*shan*) and the water (*shui*), the quintessence of which (*chi*) can be channeled into the symbolic microcosms of poetry, paintings, and garden design.

Today, however, in both the East and the West, it is debatable to what degree the aesthetics of the fine arts can apply to the broader, working landscape of contemporary culture. If beauty can be said to exist at all as an aesthetic category today, it is either relegated to history or so democratized as to be merely "in the eye of the beholder." Alternatively, as a capitalist product, beauty is an advertising device held out to lure the poor, but simultaneously rarefied as the exclusive domain of a global elite – the dominion of those who somewhat capriciously produce it and those who can simply afford it. For the rest of us the world is now predominantly ugly: the land is exploited and our cities are disfigured, nearly all of it a degraded byproduct of global, industrial modernity. Beauty is something one now visits on vacations or in museums. Against this despoliation, the environmental movement and the profession of landscape architecture valiantly uphold visions of nature as both a spiritual and aesthetic remedy, working for its preservation where it remains at least partially intact, and for its restoration where it doesn't. In the West, particularly since the dawn of the environmental movement in the 1960s, both the science of ecology and eastern spiritual traditions such as Taoism have been variously amalgamated in an effort to make whole that which the cartesian subdivision of culture and nature has so forcefully rent apart. A combination of Western rationality and Eastern holism could, it was hoped, produce a modernity without environmental destruction – in short, an ecotopia. Known in common parlance as "sustainability," this ideal society remains a beacon for landscape architects and other allied disciplines to this day.

It is ironic, then, that as the West looked to the East for ideas of holistic beauty in nature, in the late 20th century the Asian economic "tigers" looked to the West for the very opposite. Despite its deep philosophical and spiritual traditions that position humanity as a part of—instead of apart from—nature, China, especially since 1978, has exploited its own landscape with as much, if not more, industrial might than the West ever did theirs. Whereas in the West a counter-movement of conservation—and indeed the profession of landscape architecture—had time to mature alongside the historical process of industrialization, in the case of China's accelerated modernity, environmentalism and its associated aesthetics of nature have been muted and marginalized by the overwhelming national priority of lifting over a billion people out of poverty, in record time.

古希腊毕达哥拉斯神秘主义者(公元前6世纪)认为,大自然的精髓是数学,且这种精髓可以用几何图形和音乐的形式来表达。这些"形式"被柏拉图赞颂并组合成一个完整的宇宙学,且这些形式也被认为是创造并超越一切的神圣智慧的标志。这就是古希腊古典时期对美的定义,或者更确切地说,这里定义的是"绝对"美。

与此同时,在世界的另一端,虽然中国道家也认识到自然包含着一种深刻而统一的本质,并认识到它是极其美丽的。道家认为,对这种美的欣赏能带领人回归本性。然而,对希腊人来说,几何学是其心灵圣地的关键,而对道家来说,美表现在自然景观、"山"和"水"中,其中的精华("气")可以被注入诗歌、绘画和园林设计的象征性缩影之中。

然而无论在当今的东方还是西方,美术美学究竟能在多大程度上应用于当代文化里更广义、更实用的景观,仍存在争议。如果说美存在于当今的所有美学范畴之中,那么它要么被归类到历史范畴,要么被大众化到仅仅"在旁观者眼中"。或者说,作为一种资本产品,美是一种广告营销手段,旨在吸引穷人,但同时又被界定为被一些全球精英统领的专属领域,这样的精英指的是那些在某种程度上时不时地生产造就美的人,以及那些买得起美的人。对我们其他人来说,现在的世界主要是被丑陋占据的,土地被开发掠夺,城市被破坏,几乎所有这些都是全球工业现代化的副产品。如今,美变成了人们在假期或在博物馆里参观的东西。面对这种全球工业现代化的劫掠,环境运动和风景园林专业勇敢地坚持把自然视为一种精神和美学的治疗方法,努力保护自然,使其至少部分完好无损,并在其有疮痍的地方进行修复。在西方,特别是自20世纪60年代环境运动开始以来,生态学和东方精神传统(如道教)已经被融汇贯通,使被笛卡尔细分强行割裂的文化和自然重新融合成为一个整体。人们希望西方理性与东方整体主义的结合能够产生一种不破坏环境的现代性——简言之,这是一种生态乌托邦。通俗的说这也被称作是"可持续性",这个理想的社会至今仍是风景园林师和其他相关学科的灯塔。

具有讽刺意味的是,在20世纪末,当西方寻求东方的自然美理念时,亚洲经济"四小龙"却在寻求西方的与自然美相斥的美学理念。尽管中国有着深厚的哲学与精神文化传统,认为人类是自然的一部分,而不是与自然分离

西方景观"美"的经典例子，摄于英国斯图尔黑德帕
Stourhead, England – a classic example of Western landscape "beauty"

割裂。但是放眼中国，尤其是自1978年以来，中国已经比西方国家更多地利用了工业力量来开发自己的景观。而在西方，有一种属于风景园林专业范畴的反向保护运动，这种运动仍需要时间，需要随着工业化的历史进程逐渐成熟。中国持续加速的现代化、环保主义及其相关的自然美学相比于国家创纪录地让超过十亿人摆脱了贫困这一压倒性的壮举，却显得无人问津且边缘化。

令人赞叹着迷的是，中国政府在大力推进现代化和城市化的同时，还同时启动了国家政策，不仅要建设一个富裕的中国，而且要建设一个"美丽中国"。尽管这可能意味着许多流于表面或强制性的东西，但让"美丽中国"这个概念最引人注目的是，它被囊括在习近平总主席所说的创造"生态文明"的更大理念之中。2013年，他郑重宣布，中国必须从GDP文明转向生态文明。换句话说，中国的国家领导人实际上刚刚宣告了一个生态乌托邦的黎明，中国正迅速成为21世纪全球最卓越的超级大国。

当然，"美丽中国"这一国家政策需要风景园林行业做出回应。然而，在查阅了相关文献，并与中国同行交谈

It is fascinating, then, that even while still in the midst of intense modernization and urbanization, the Chinese government has simultaneously launched the national policy of creating not just a wealthy China, but also a "Beautiful China." Whereas this could mean any number of superficial and/or oppressive things, what makes the idea of Beautiful China most compelling is that it is nested within the even bigger idea of what President Xi Jinping refers to as the creation of "ecological civilization." China, Xi momentously declared in 2013, must move from a GDP civilization to an ecological civilization. In other words, the President of China has effectively just declared the dawn of an ecotopia in what is fast becoming the world's preeminent 21st-century superpower.

Surely, then, the national policy of Beautiful China calls upon the profession of landscape architecture to respond. However, after reviewing the literature and speaking with Chinese colleagues, what exactly is meant by Beautiful China and ecological civilization is unclear. Perhaps, like all great political rhetoric, these expressions can mean

《富春山居图》 黄公望

*Dwelling in the Fuchun Mountains* by Huang Gongwang – a classic example of Chinese landscape "beauty"

all things to all people. Perhaps, because both beauty and ecology mean a lot that is specific to landscape architecture, it is for landscape architects to translate the rhetoric into reality. Could it be, then, that the Chinese government just delivered the profession of landscape architecture its greatest mandate – one that, at least since McHarg, the profession has routinely claimed it deserves? And if so, how will the discipline and profession now respond? How should the discipline and profession respond?

With funding from the University of Pennsylvania's China Research and Engagement Fund (CREF), this was the question we asked of a leading group of Chinese landscape architecture academics at the Beautiful China Symposium convened at the Chinese Academy of Fine Art (CAFA) in Beijing in March 2019. For the symposium we asked both established and emerging academics to present their research in the light of Beautiful China and, importantly, as we hope this volume reflects, our intention was to facilitate not lead the discussion. To bring the relationship between

之后,"美丽中国"和"生态文明"究竟是什么意思还并不明确。也许,就像所有伟大的政治辞令一样,这样的表达对所有人来说都是包罗万象的。也许,因为美和生态对风景园林都有特殊的意义,所以风景园林师应该把这些修辞转化为现实。那么,中国政府是否刚刚赋予风景园林这个职业最大的使命呢?至少自麦克·哈格以来,风景园林行业一直声称自己理应担当起这个使命?如果风景园林师肩负起了这个使命,那么风景园林在学科及专业层面上将怎样回应,应当怎样回应?

在宾夕法尼亚大学中国研究与参与基金(CREF)的支持下,我们于2019年3月在中国美术学院(CAFA)举办的"美丽中国"研讨会上向中国风景园林学界的一批领军人提出了这个问题。在研讨会上,我们邀请了资深学者和新晋学者,以"美丽中国"为蓝本介绍他们的研究成果。重要的是,正如我们希望本书所反映的那样,我们旨在促进而非引导讨论。通过美来聚焦人与土地的关系,尤其是在一个土地与身份长期紧密相连的文化中并不是一件小事。正如我们很快了解到的,"美丽中国"是通往迷宫的一扇门,迷宫中充满了有关当代中国身份文化认同的复杂而敏感的问题。

本书所收录的论文的内容，基本都是在“美丽中国”论坛上探讨过的。这些论文涵盖广泛的主题，如政策分析、设计理论、社区参与和环境规划。除了我们的中国同行的论文，我在宾夕法尼亚大学的同事玛丽莲·乔丹·泰勒（Marilyn Taylor）和克里斯多夫·马辛考斯基(Christopher Marcinkoski)一直都在积极从事与中国相关的专业和学术活动，他们对城市设计问题的思考研究也被囊括在本书内。由于时间和篇幅的限制，我们请各位作者简短地探讨他们对专业的思考，他们的文章也确实比较简短。因此，重要的是，本书只是相关议题的开始而不是结束。

这本书是过去四年来在宾夕法尼亚大学中国研究与参与基金(CREF)的中美跨文化交流基金项目的支持下所开展的一系列活动的成果。例如，与其他同事，如建筑领域的阿里·拉一姆(Ali Rahim)、美术领域的林俭（Ken Lum）和历史保护领域的兰迪·梅森（Randy Mason）一起，我们开展了各种不同的主题、场地和规模的设计课、研讨会和工作坊。例如，我们对北京作为京津冀大都市中心的未来以及2050年深圳的情况开展了设计课进行研究探讨。在完全不同的另一种尺度之下，我们仔细推敲研究了当代中国园林的细节，同时参加了南头城中村的都市主义与建筑深港双年展。我们还在北京宾夕法尼亚沃顿中国中心举办了一场盛大的当代建筑展览，与此同时我们与历史保护方向的学者举行了圆桌会议，与开发商和主要城市规划者举办了城市设计论坛。所有这些活动都得到了宾夕法尼亚大学的支持，同时我们也很感谢AECOM对我们一直以来的额外支持。

在2015年至2019年的这波生态文明热潮中，中国学生重点把这些项目作为学习的一部分。但不只止步于此类项目。因为对他们来说，在这些项目中提出的问题往往是很有个人针对性的，这给我们的工作增加了一种特殊的强度与压力，并且每个参与的人也都因这一进程而得到充实。宾夕法尼亚大学长期以来一直是中国学生学习设计的理想之地，我们很荣幸能够教授这一代的中国学生。

本书中穿插着郑盛远同学拍摄的照片。盛远的任务是游历中国，为这本书的每一篇文章捕捉拍摄相关照片，同时也反映出他自己的愿景。最近毕业于宾夕法尼亚大学的张晨笛和蔡伊凡主要负责本书的作者签约、论文和文稿的翻译以及本书的平面设计。晨笛和伊凡也为本书

people and land into focus through the lens of beauty—especially in a culture where land and identity have been so tightly coupled for so long—is no small matter. As we quickly learned, Beautiful China is a door to a labyrinth of complicated and sensitive issues regarding contemporary Chinese identity.

Collected in this volume are the papers more or less as they were presented by the speakers at the Beautiful China Symposium. The essays range widely across topics such as policy analysis, design theory, community engagement, and environmental planning. In addition to the contributions from our Chinese peers, short reflections on matters of urban design by our University of Pennsylvania colleagues Marilyn Taylor and Christopher Marcinkoski (both of whom have been actively engaged professionally and academically in China) are included. Constrained by both time and space, we asked our colleagues to be brief in their deliberations and they have obliged. Accordingly, it is important to note that this volume is a beginning, not an end.

This book is the culmination of a range of activities conducted over the last four years under the aegis of The University of Pennsylvania's CREF program of cross-cultural engagement with China. Along with colleagues in architecture (Ali Rahim), city planning (Marilyn Taylor and Robert Yaro), fine arts (Ken Lum), and historic preservation (Randy Mason), we have conducted design studios, seminars, and workshops across a wide range of topics, sites, and scales. For example, we have run interdisciplinary design studios on the future of Beijing as the center of the Jing-Jin-Ji megaregion, on what Shenzhen might be like in the year 2050, and the aesthetics of contemporary Chinese gardens. We participated in the Bi-City Biennale of Urbanism and Architecture in the migrant workers' village of Nantou, and we held a major exhibition of contemporary architecture at the Penn Wharton China Center in Beijing. We have held roundtables with historic preservationists and urban design forums with developers and leading urban planners. All this activity has been supported by the University of Pennsylvania, but we are also grateful to AECOM for their additional and ongoing patronage.

In this flurry of activity between 2015 and 2019 it was mainly, but not only, Chinese students who took on these projects as part of their studies. Because for them the questions being asked in these projects were often personal, it has given our work a particular intensity and everyone involved has been enriched by the process. The University of Pennsylvania has long been a highly desirable place for Chinese students to study design and for us it is an honor to teach this new generation of Chinese students.

This book is interleaved with images taken by one such student, Shengyuan Zheng. Shengyuan's brief was to travel through China and compose photographs related to each essay in this book, whilst also reflecting his own vision. Recent Penn landscape architecture graduates Chendi Zhang and Yifan Cai have been responsible for author engagement, translation of essays and documents, and the graphic design of this book. Chendi and Yifan were also instrumental in the success of the Beautiful China Symposium from which this book arises. Closing the book, as he did the original symposium, is an afterword by one of the world's leading theorists of Chinese gardens, Stanislaus Fung of the Chinese University of Hong Kong.

This book is dedicated to our Chinese colleagues and students. It is intended as both a catalyst for and a championing of the growing importance of landscape architecture in China today.

Richard J. Weller and Tatum L. Hands

的前身，即“美丽中国论坛”的成功举办发挥了重要作用。这本书的结束语是由香港中文大学的冯仕达教授撰写的，他曾在之前的论坛上做了闭幕陈词，同时他也是世界领先的中国园林理论家之一。

仅以书献给我们的中国同行和学生们。本书旨在促进与支持风景园林在当今中国日益增长的重要地位。

理查德·J·韦勒与泰特姆·L·汉兹

文化鼎觀

# 文化景观
# The Cultural Landscape

# Beautiful China and the Mission of Landscape Architecture
# 美丽中国与景观学的担当

**俞孔监** | YU Kongjian

Professor, College of Architecture and Landscape, Peking University and founder and design principal of Turenscape. Yu holds a doctorate of design from Harvard University Graduate School of Design where he was a visiting professor from 2010–2015. He is author of 25 books and his ecologically and culturally sensitive projects have won numerous international design awards. Yu received an honorary doctorate from the Sapienza University of Rome in 2017.

北京大学建筑与景观设计学院教授，同时也是北京土人城市规划设计股份有限公司的创始人。他拥有哈佛大学设计学博士学位，同时在2010-2015年间成为哈佛大学访问教授。他编写了25本专业书籍，并通过他对于生态文化敏感区的研究与设计项目获得了无数的国际设计大奖。并在2017年被罗马大学授予名誉博士学位。

Beautiful China is a concept full of magic; it depicts an ideal society and its environment. As a "Chinese Dream" that 1.4 billion people are now pursuing, it dates back to the report of the 18th National Congress of the Communist Party of China on November 8, 2012, which declared:

> "Building an ecological civilization is a matter of people's well-being and a long-term plan for the future. Facing the situation of resource constraints, environmental pollution, and degraded ecosystems, we must establish an ecological civilization that respects nature, adapts to nature, and protects nature, and puts ecological civilization construction in a prominent position and integrates it into the whole process of economic, political, cultural, and social construction so as to build a beautiful China and realize the sustainable development of the Chinese nation."

What is interesting is that this ideal, put forward by the Communist Party of China as a goal of socialist China, is now being discussed by an American university – the University of Pennsylvania School of Design! Such discussions are challenging but extremely exciting. The announcement for the PennDesign-sponsored Beautiful China Symposium in Beijing stated: "The purpose is to establish a platform for discussing landscape architecture in China in relation

to the concept of Beautiful China in a global context." This discussion is indeed very meaningful and valuable; it requires us to clarify the relationship between landscape architecture and the concept of Beautiful China, and to understand this relationship at a specific operational level so that the academy and profession can serve the goals of the Beautiful China concept. Specifically, we must answer three key questions. First, what is Beautiful China and what is its relationship to the national land and landscape? Second, what kind of China is beautiful and how do we evaluate beauty? And third, how do we achieve Beautiful China through the practice of landscape architecture?

From the original source, we can see that the essence of Beautiful China is a depiction of an ideal social form, which can be expressed as a social form of economic prosperity, political rectitude, cultural richness, social equity, and human–nature harmony. In this sense, Beautiful China obviously goes far beyond the study of landscape architecture. That said, landscape architecture is directly implicated in the realization of Beautiful China because,

"美丽中国"是一个充满魔力的概念，是一个理想社会及其存在空间的形态。作为一个14亿人民奋斗的"中国梦"，其完整的诠释应该回到2012年11月8日，中国共产党第十八次全国代表大会的报告："建设生态文明，是关系人民福祉、关乎民族未来的长远大计。面对资源约束趋紧、环境污染严重、生态系统退化的严峻形势，必须树立尊重自然、顺应自然、保护自然的生态文明理念，把生态文明建设放在突出地位，融入经济建设、政治建设、文化建设、社会建设各方面和全过程，努力建设美丽中国，实现中华民族永续发展。"

非常有意思的是，这个由中国共产党提出来、作为社会主义中国建设目标的伟大理想，今天却由美国的大学机构，宾夕法尼亚大学设计学院来主持讨论！这样的讨论充满挑战却极其令人振奋。发起人在其对外发布的公告说："其目的是为世界景观设计学的讨论以及在全球背景下讨论中国的景观设计学，尤其是服务于美丽中国建设的景观设计学建立一个平台。"从这个意义上说，这确是一个非常有意义和值得深入探讨的课题，它需要我们明确设计学科、特别是景观学与美丽中国的关系，在具体的操作性层面上认识它、理解它，并使我们的学术和实践能为之服务。具体的说，我们必须明确三个方面的问题：美丽中国是什么，它与国土空间和景观有何关系？什么样的中国是美丽的，其评价标准是什么？如何来实现美丽中国，景观学的途径是什么？

首先，美丽中国是美好的社会形态及其在大地上的投影。从原始出处中，我们所以看到，美丽中国实质是一种理想社会形态的描绘，可以表述为经济繁荣、政治清明、文化昌盛、社会公平和谐的理想社会形态。显然，这个意义上的美丽中国远远超出了景观学的研究范畴。景观学关心的是物质空间上的美丽中国。所幸的是，景观学的理论告诉我们，物质的景观形态恰恰是社会形态的投影和折射[1]。当然，反过来，美丽的景观影响人们的行为乃至社会形态，即所谓一方水土养一方人，穷山恶水出刁民。战乱频繁、贫富不均、不讲法治的社会，必然是遍地高墙深壑，鸟兽绝迹；一个贪腐泛滥，暴民横行，是非不分，黑白颠倒的社会，必然污水横流，垃圾遍地。有了清明和谐的社会，便会有绿水青山之大地。反之也然，桃花源的美丽，孕育了桃花源中人的夜不闭户、怡然自得的社会形态。从这个意义上说，营造美丽中国，景观设计学当仁不让。

第二，什么样的中国是美丽的，其评价标准是什么？这恰恰是美丽中国建设能否成功的关键。君不见，遍中国大地的丑陋景观，都是在"美丽"的名义下规划设计和实施出来的，诸如城市中畸形怪状的建筑，令人啼笑皆非的巨型广场和霓虹灯闪烁的"景观大道"，绵延几十公里甚至几百公里的渠化、硬化的河流，偏僻乡村的汉白玉河道和"金水桥"、"天安门"，城市种满大街从乡下移栽来的奇花异木、古树名木和太湖石，节庆广场上的龙形和凤形花坛，等等，不一而足。在美化的名义下，我们毁掉了大地的生态与自然之美，乡村的质朴与丰产之美，城市的文化与生活之美。所以，有了美丽中国建设的号角，我们尚需要有一个关于美的标准的顶层设计，也就是需要有一个主流的审美价值体系，来引导美丽中国建设的实践。中国几千年的封建主流文化中，就有近2000年的以"小脚"为美的士大夫主流审美观，因此，遍中国良家妇女皆以裹足为美。畸形和病态的小脚被作为高雅与美的标准，病态之美因此而泛滥牺牲健康、不事生产、残缺畸形、表里不一、无病呻吟、扭捏作态。这种审美观注定是不可持续的！因此，必须回归健康、寻常的"大脚之美，"它将还疾病缠身的中

as Denis Cosgrove has explained, the material world is precisely the projection and refraction of social forms.[1] In turn, the form of the landscape can also affect people's individual behavior and society's collective form.

There is a Chinese expression that different environments give different characteristics to their residents – bad environments create ugly people, beautiful mountains and waters nurture good people. A society with frequent wars, corruption, and inequality will be a place with high fences and no trace of vitality, a place with open sewers and garbage everywhere. In contrast, the utopic image of the "land of peach blossoms" (paradise in Chinese culture) invokes an equal and harmonious society, a place with vast green land and clear blue water. In this sense, landscape architecture has a central role in building a beautiful China.

We must ask then what kind of China is beautiful, and by what criteria do we measure this beauty? This is the key to achieving the successful construction of Beautiful China. Sadly, most of the ugly landscapes of China are designed and constructed in the name of beauty: countless odd buildings in the cities, ridiculous giant plazas, and huge boulevards blazing with neon light. Tens, or even hundreds, of thousands of kilometers of channelized river are built with lifeless hard riverbanks; marble paving and fake Tiananmen Squares are built in remote villages; exotic ornamental plants, deformed ancient trees, and Taihu rocks are shipped thousands of miles from villages to beautify cities; and shrubs are trimmed into the shapes of dragons and phoenixes to decorate central squares.

In the name of such superficial beautification, we ruin the real beauty of the ecosystem and the nature of our land, the beauty of the countryside's simplicity, authenticity, and richness, and the beauty of the city's cultural life. Therefore, along with the call for the creation of Beautiful China, we also need a top-down specification of the criteria of beauty; which is to say, we need a mainstream aesthetic value system to guide the construction of Beautiful China. For example, for two thousand years in China there has been an aesthetic of admiring females' "small feet." In pursuit

宿迁三台山衲田花海

Suqian Santaishan flower quilt

of this gentrification, women from all over China had their feet bound, sacrificing their health and their ability to work. This aesthetic is destined not to last. We must return to the healthy and ordinary aesthetic of "the big feet," which will restore the beauty of health, the beauty of nature, and the beauty of fertility, and return authenticity to the Chinese countryside and cities that are "ugly-ridden." The beauty of the healthy big feet is precisely the beauty of Beautiful China and the beauty of ecological civilization that has been proposed by China's leaders. It is a beauty with depth, a beauty which infuses human desire with the concepts of ecology and sustainability.

As President Xi Jinping has said "clear waters and green mountains are as good as mountains of gold and silver." This logic establishes the unity of the desires for a better life, for a beautiful China, and for a safe and healthy environment. These desires depend upon the existence of high-quality ecosystem services, which in turn depend upon China securing the ecological integrity of its landscapes. And this is also the stage where Chinese landscape architecture can show its talents.

国城乡以生机勃勃的健康之美、生态之美、丰产之美、乡土而朴实之美。这样的"大脚之美，"正是中国最高决策层所提出的生态文明建设理念的美丽中国，是一种"深邃之形"，一种将人类的欲望建立在生态和可持续理念之上的美。

这种大脚之美的核心是关于自然所提供的生态系统服务(ecosystem services)是人类福祉的来源的认识论和价值观。人民对美好生活的向往，本质上是高品质的生态系统服务，包括供给服务、生命承载、调节服务和精神文化服务。它们是人与自然之间和谐关系的纽带，也是"绿水青山就是金山银山"(习近平语)的根本逻辑所在。这一逻辑确立了"人对美好生活的向往——美丽中国——高品质的生态系统服务——安全和健康的国土生态系统(景观)"之间的统一关系。所以，美丽中国的标准就是高品质的生态系统服务，而高品质的生态系统服务有赖于能持续提供这些服务的自然之"大脚"——在国土空间有限条件下、对维护生态过程具有关键意义的生态安全格局和以生态安全格局为核心的生态基础设施。而这正是中国景观学将可以大显身手的地方。

第三，如何来实现美丽中国，美丽中国的景观学途径是什么？

因此，规划和设计美丽中国的“深邃之形”——具有高品质的生态服务、人与自然和谐共生的景观，是景观学在美丽中国建设中的首要、也是核心的任务。而景观学的本质是人类改造自然、协调人与自然关系的学问。从发生学的角度来说，人与自然的关系都是由于人的出现，改变了自然原有的生态系统。这种改变或是和谐的，或是冲突的，和谐或冲突的程度一方面取决于人类对自然改变或干扰的强度，另一方面也取决于自然生态系统本身的韧性。由此，我们来定义生态文明理念下的美丽及其形态：建立在自然生态系统的韧性基础上的人类改造自然的活动及其创造的形态。也就是说，美丽中国是与自然相适应的中国人改造世界的活动及其创造的物质和社会形态。这就回到了“劳动创造了人”和“劳动创造美”这一命题。正是人类为生存而进行的改造自然、改造社会的劳动，才是人类得以进化的根本动力，也是推动人类社会进步的根本动力。从这个意义上来说，美丽中国便是中国人民的“生存的艺术[2]。”

从人类改造自然而创造美丽的角度出发，也就是景观学的角度，生态文明理念下的美丽中国的形态需要从三个层面来营造：美丽的构形（configurative form）、美丽的变形（transformative form）及美丽的行为本身（beautiful behavior）。这三者构成了美丽的深邃之形[3]。

美丽的构型（configurative beautiful form）：人与自然的空间毗邻关系而形成的格局。由于人的活动的介入使自然的空间格局发生改变，这种改变首先体现在人与自然的空间关系上，即人与自然之间必须划出一条界限，来表征两者的空间关系。人与自然相互作用的人类生态系统是多尺度的，从一个家园、到城市、区域和整个国土，通过跨尺度的自然保护空间的划定，保障自然生态系统结构和过程的完整性和连续性。如河流廊道的边界，自然保护区的边界，明确人类活动与自然之间的分界线，通过这条边界（生态红线、底线等）的划定，确定了人与自然关系的空间格局。美丽的格局就是人与自然的界限是否划得合理，是否各自都有空间，两者的碰撞是否具有韧性和余地。

This leads to the question, how can landscape architects best help achieve Beautiful China? Planning and designing the landscape with high-quality ecological services must work with the deep form of the landscape and strive to create a harmonious coexistence between humanity and nature. This is the primary task of landscape architecture in the construction of Beautiful China. The essence of landscape architecture lies in knowledge about how humans interact with and change the natural environment. This change can be either harmonious or conflicting, and the degree of harmony or conflict depends on the extent of humanity's disturbance of natural ecosystems. On the other hand, it also depends on the resilience of the natural ecosystem itself. From this understanding, we can define the beauty and form of the concept of ecological civilization as the sum total of the activities of human transformation of the land that are based on the resilience of natural ecosystems. In other words, Beautiful China is an activity that transforms the world through adaption of nature. It is the material and social forms of this activity. This meaning returns to the manifesto of Marxism that "labor creates people" and "labor creates beauty," the labor of transforming nature and society for human survival is the fundamental driving force for human evolution and the advancement of human society. In this sense, Beautiful China is the "art of survival" of the Chinese people.[2]

The form of Beautiful China under the overarching concept of ecological civilization needs to be created on three levels: configurative beautiful form, transformative beautiful form, and beautiful behavior. These three together constitute what I refer to as beautiful deep form.[3]

Configurative beautiful form is a pattern depicting the boundary drawn between humanity and nature to characterize the spatial relationship between the two, it is the main task of spatial planning of our national land. The ecosystem in which humans interact with nature must be considered at multiple scales—home, city, region, nation—through the delineation of natural conservation spaces to ensure the integrity and continuity of natural ecosystem structures and ecological processes. For example, through the delineation of boundaries

三亚红树林生态公园
Sanya Mangrove Park

美丽的变形(transformative beautiful form):景观的第二种形态体现在人与自然之间的第二种关系中,即两者在空间上的叠加关系,或是融合的关系。在许多情况下,人类活动和自然之间没法划定明确的边界。如梯田是人类文化的产物,但它是离不开自然基底和自然过程而存在的,它是文化与自然的叠加而产生的形状。在生态文明的理念下,这种形状是否美丽,取决于人类的文化活动是否适应于自然的地形、水文、营养流和物种的生长规律。也就是人类的改造活动是否与自然过程相适应。在这里,人与自然和谐的形状,也就是美丽的形状就如纸张下的硬币在铅笔涂抹后留在纸上的图案。

美丽的行为(beautiful behavior):是指与资源诉求相关联的人类生产生活方式。尽管这方面并不是物质空间的规划设计的核心内容,但无处不体现在景观的设计、改造、使用及管理的各个方面。人类为满足自己的欲望而进行的生产生活过程,在更深层面上决定了人与自然的关系。人与自然和谐的行为方式,也就是美丽的标准,体现在通过节制欲望、提高效率和减少污染,来管理人类对资源的诉求或对环境的冲击,另一方面,也通过明智地协调人的活动与自然之间的空间格局关系以及人与自然之间的空间叠加关系来引导人类的生产生活方式和行为。

构型、变形和行为三个层面相互联系、共同作用,构成了一个完整的、景观学介入美丽中国建设的操作界面和行动路径。景观作为社会形态在大地上的投影,以及景观对人类行为和社会的反作用,注定使景观学将成为美丽中国建设的中坚。也正因为如为此,中国城市科学研究会于2017年发起成立了“景观学与美丽中国建设专业委员会,”并提出宣言:“天降大任!景观设计师具有独特的优势,使其能将相关专业联合一起,形成新的联盟来应对复杂生态和环境问题。我们坚信,只要深刻认识到地球系统的复杂性和整体性,认识到人类活动与自然系统之间需要和谐调理,通过的整体的功能协调和艺术的设计,重建美丽和谐的新桃源:从国土和区域,到城市和乡村。当前最紧迫的任务是国土生态重建、城市修补和生态修复、海绵城市建设以及广大乡村的保护和建设[4]。”

between human activities and nature—such as the boundary of a river corridor or the boundary of a nature reserve—the spatial pattern of the relationship between humanity and nature is determined. The pattern’s beauty is determined by whether the boundary between humanity and nature is reasonable, and whether there is resilient and adaptive space where they directly interact with each other.

Transformative beautiful form arises where humanity and nature are superimposed in space and time so that a new hybrid emerges. In these cases, there is no clear boundary between human activities and nature. For example, an agricultural terrace is a product of human culture, but it cannot exist without its natural base and natural processes. It is formed by the superimposition of culture and nature. With the concept of ecological civilization, whether this form is beautiful depends on the degree to which the original natural form and integrity of ecological processes are respected and included in the transformative design. In this sense, the form of harmony and beauty between humanity and nature is like the pattern of coins left on the paper after a pencil is applied on top.

Beautiful behavior, the third dimension of beautiful deep form, refers to the human use of natural resources for survival. Although this aspect is not the core content of the planning and design of material space, it is ubiquitous in all aspects of landscape design, transformation, use, and management. The production and living processes that human beings carry out to satisfy their own desires determines the relationship between humanity and nature at a deeper level. The harmony between humans and nature—that is, the standard of beauty—is reflected in managing human desires for resources or their impact on the environment by controlling desires, improving efficiency, and reducing pollution.

These three levels of configuration, transformation, and behavior interact and work together to form a complete operational interface for landscape architecture studies to engage with the construction of Beautiful China. As the projection of the social form on the land, landscape architecture is destined to become the backbone of the construction of Beautiful China.

As a conclusion, I would like to quote the manifesto declared by the Landscape Architecture and Beautiful China Committee of the Chinese Society for Urban Studies upon its establishment in 2017:

> "There is a great responsibility for landscape architecture! Landscape architects have a unique advantage in coordinating all the relevant professions to form new alliances to deal with current complex ecological and environmental issues. We firmly believe that, as long as we are deeply aware of the complexity and integrity of the Earth system, and recognize the need for harmonious coordination between human activities and natural systems, with holistic functional coordination and artistic design, we can rebuild a beautiful and harmonious new land of peach blossoms ranging from the nation, the region, the cities, to the countryside."[4]

1. Cosgrove D., *Social Formation and Symbolic Landscape* (Wisconsin: University of Wisconsin Press, 1998).
2. Yu K., *The Art of Survival: Positioning Landscape Architecture* (China Architecture & Building Press, 2006).
3. Yu K., "Creating Deep Forms in Urban Nature: The peasant's approach to urban design," in Steiner, F.R., Thompson G.F. & Carbonell A. (eds), *Nature and Cities – The Ecological Imperative in Urban Design and Planning* (Lincoln Institute of Land Policy, 2016), 95–117.
4. Landscape Architecture and Beautiful China Committee, Chinese Society for Urban Studies, "Declaration of Landscape Architecture in China" (2017).

# The Philosophy behind Beautiful China

## 美丽中国——融合人与自然，创建诗意栖居

**韩锋 | HAN Feng**

Professor and Chair, Department of Landscape Architecture, Tongji University. Han holds a Bachelor and Master of Landscape Architecture from Tongji University, and a PhD from Queensland University of Technology, Australia. She is Vice President of ICOMOS-IFLA International Scientific Committee on Cultural Landscapes, an expert member of the IUCN World Commission on Protected Areas, and founder and Chair of the Cultural Landscape Committee of the Chinese Society of Landscape Architecture. Her research and practice are focused on heritage cultural landscape conservation and management.

教授，同济大学建筑与城市规划学院景观学系系主任，博士生导师。同济大学风景园林学士、硕士，澳大利亚昆士兰科技大学风景园林哲学博士。联合国教科文世界遗产咨询机构——国际古迹遗址理事会-国际风景园林师联合会文化景观科学委员会（ICOMOS-IFLA ISCCL）副主席，主持亚太区工作；国际自然保护联盟(IUCN)世界保护地委员会（WCPA）专家；中国风景园林学会文化景观专业委员会主任委员。韩锋教授的理论研究与实践一直聚焦于全球化和城市化语境下的文化景观遗产的保护和管理、跨文化比较及环境伦理等领域。

The Beautiful China proposal is a country's ideal and dream for the future. It is China's expectation for a new era, a determination to change the current situation, and a political decision to shape the future. In order to move from an agricultural and industrial civilization to an ecological civilization, China is devoted to reconstructing a harmonious human–nature relationship. The construction of Beautiful China within the larger framework of an ecological civilization is at its core consistent with the goal of landscape architecture: to deal with the root of environmental problems and to realize the dream of human beings and nature living poetically together on the earth.

Beautiful China was proposed as a national policy in 2012. After more than 30 years of rapid development, China's urbanization rate reached 50% in 2011; but, to this end, China has paid a high environmental cost. Environmental crises such as water and soil pollution and ecosystem degradation increased significantly. In the face of severe environmental conditions and unprecedented human–nature conflicts, the central government demanded change in environmental values, and to rebuild a sustainable human–nature relationship. This requires us to respect nature, adapt to nature, and protect nature in all aspects of the economic, political, cultural, and social development process. The concept of ecological civilization promotes the comprehensive formation of green development methods and lifestyles, and seeks to build a beautiful China in which humankind and nature live in harmony.

Beautiful China is not a "shallow ecology" movement, concerned with pollution and resource depletion; rather, it is a "deep ecology" movement characterized metaphysically, ethically, and politically.[1] It holds an anti-anthropocentric position and calls for a revolutionary philosophical reexamination of human–nature relations and repositioning of human and natural values. It concerns the sustainability of humankind and the earth and has far-reaching historical influence on the future of the discipline of landscape architecture.

First, Beautiful China requires a new human attitude to nature and the construction of a new value system of nature. Is nature intrinsically valuable? What is the beauty of nature? Is the "natural beauty" that we appreciate scientific or humanistic? Do we have the responsibility and ability to acknowledge and respect the intrinsic values of nature? These are new challenges raised by the new era. For a country like China, while we are admiring the beauty of China's splendid cultural landscape underpinned by deep philosophical traditions of the unity of nature and human, we also need to reflect on such cultural

美丽中国——这个口号在中国的提出，是一个国家对未来的理想和梦想，是中国对于一个新时代到来的期望，是对于改变当下命运的决心，是目标和方向的决策。中国要从农业文明、工业文明光荣和危机中，走向生态文明，完成新型人地关系的重新建构。以生态文明为核心的"美丽中国"建设，与风景园林的学科目标是一致的：实现人类与自然共同诗意地栖息于大地的梦想。

以"生态文明"建设为核心的"美丽中国"是中国在2012年提出的国策，中国的城市化建设，在经历了30余年高速发展后，在2011年达到了50%的城市化率，但为此付出了高昂的环境代价，水土污染、生态系统退化等各种环境问题聚集性爆发，人地关系面临着空前危机和冲突。面对严峻的环境形势，中央要求转变环境价值观念，重建人地关系，以生态文明建设为中心，在经济、政治、文化、社会建设各方面和全过程，体现尊重自然、顺应自然、保护自然的生态文明理念，促进绿色发展方式和生活方式的全面形成，建成人与自然和谐共生的美丽中国。

表面上看，这是一场治理生态污染的运动。实质上，是一场从根本上扭转自然价值观，重新确立人与自然关系的环境哲学运动，是一场环境哲学的“深生态”革命运动[1]，事关人与自然的和谐持续发展，对风景园林学科的发展具有深远的历史性影响。

首先，建设生态文明需要在环境哲学基础上重建自然价值体系。在人与自然的关系中，“自然美”是自然的还是人文的？自然是否具有独立于人之外的、内在的美学价值？我们是否能够并且应当真正承认、认知和尊重自然内在的科学价值和科学美？这是新时代对所有人的自然科学观、环境伦理观提出的新问题。对于中国这样一个具有“天人合一”自然观的国家，在赞叹“天人合一”带来中国灿烂文化景观之美的同时，需要冷静地分析、反思由于人与自然主客不分而带来的文化影响以及对自然科学价值的长期轻视，自然的科学价值认知和保护刻不容缓，对人类生命之外自然生命福祉的伦理及科学价值关注急需提高。

第二，对于“美丽”的意义层次的理解。景观是由文化族群创造，是社会的建构产物。人们对事物的“美丽”感受，与对事物的知识、情感、信仰、解说密切相关，对事物意义的理解决定了客体在主体的“美丽”感知映射程度。景观对象和作品重要的是视觉形式美？还是对景观的意义理解？我们是否具备阅读景观意义，并将这种意义转化为我们景观作品深度价值观的能力？“美丽”的关注重点和思想深刻性决定着我们风景园林学科的“美丽”价值取向。

第三，对“美丽”的社会与文化话语权的思考。谁决定是否“美丽”？我们需要什么样的“美丽”？我们需要去创造和保护谁眼中的“美丽”？“美丽”如何体现文化多样性和社会公平公正性？中国快速城市化的过程中，正在兴起一场乡村振兴、脱贫致富的运动，城市和乡村的景观在发生着巨大的变化。景观作为与主体情感、记忆、信仰高度相关的社会空间，体现着社会对自然资源和空间资源的分配的公平和公正，是社会权力分配的真实反映，具有高度的社会性。“乡愁”、“美丽乡村”不仅仅是文化记忆、建筑符号，更是乡村千家万户的安心栖居之地。当前中国“美丽乡村”建设中出现的问题，把乡村作为城市后花园，把供城市居民消费乡村景观的旅游民宿作为乡村发展的万灵药，建设城里人眼中的“美丽”的“舞台化”乡村，农田抛荒，把农民变成乡村旅游服务人口，在乡村培育了新一批的城

influence of the inseparability between people and nature on the long-term contempt for scientific natural values. Recognition of the scientific values of nature and the protection of well-being beyond human life must urgently be improved.

Second, Beautiful China needs to strengthen its understanding of the layering of meanings of “beauty.” Is beauty the visual form or the meaning of the landscape? Do we have the ability to read the meaning of the landscape and translate it into the value of our landscape work and interpret it for others? From a cultural landscape perspective, landscape is the product of social construction. People’s feelings about beauty are closely related to their knowledge, emotions, and beliefs about the landscape. Their understanding of the world determines the degree of beauty that is perceived by the subject from the object. The focus and the meaning of beauty differs from community to community. The profundity of the understanding of beauty forms the value system of the landscape architecture discipline.

Third, we should think about the cultural power of beauty. Who decides whether something is “beautiful”? What kind of beauty do we need? Whose beauty do we need to create and protect? How does beauty reflect cultural diversity and social equity? As part of Beautiful China, the “Beautiful Rural” movement to revitalize China’s rural areas and eradicate poverty has been evolving. Urban and rural landscapes are undergoing tremendous change. As a social space highly related to subjective emotions, memories, and beliefs, landscape also reflects the social power of distribution of natural and spatial resources. At present, the countryside is regarded as the back garden and the rural landscape is constructed as a static, staged, beautiful, picturesque commodity for city people to consume. Farmland has been abandoned. Rural tourism has become a panacea for rural poverty. Farmers are turning into rural tourism service providers while city people become a new batch of urban upstarts in the countryside, reflecting the inequality of urban and rural areas and the weakness of the rural economy. Such changes fundamentally denied the value of the rural landscape and its creators, and caused the rapid disappearance of rural landscape and rural economy.

"Beautiful Rural" is key to China's urbanization. Thus, in the future, the thinking of rural beauty is likely to expand to the value of rural landscape as heritage, the wisdom to survive and live on the land and to maintain biocultural diversity in the framework of the sustainable development of society, politics, economy, culture, and environment. Rural beauty should have its own beauty, instead of always being given "beautiful" values by the city.

Fourth, it is necessary to clarify the relationship between the current ideas of beauty and Chinese historical aesthetics. The contemporary creation of beauty requires both tradition and innovation. Landscape is the habitat of culture. It records the history of different cultural groups' experience, scientific cognition, cultural practice, and the ideal pursuit of nature with collective memories and identities. Landscape is humanistic, but also scientific; it is not only a history of human culture but also a scientific history of human understanding of nature, a precious legacy of human society and nation. History needs to evolve from the past, not break with it. It is a regret that the environment we are changing, the beauty

市新贵，反映了城乡话语权的不平等、乡村经济的弱势，从根本上否定了乡村景观及其创造者的价值，并导致了真实的、美丽的、乡村景观和乡村经济的急剧消失。"美丽乡村"的建设，是中国进一步城市化的关键所在，乡村的价值，急需在社会、政治、经济、文化和环境的可持续发展框架中得到明确和认识，并与城市一起，共同创造集体记忆和转型，而不总是被城市给与和制造其"美丽"的价值。

第四，对于"中国式美丽"的理解。"美丽中国"是具有国家、地区的身份认同和文化识别性的，需要明确现时的"美丽"与中国历史传统的关系，既需要传承历史，又需要创新发展。景观是文化的栖息地，真实地记录着不同文化族群对自然的经验认知、科学认知、文化实践及理想追求的历史轨迹，记录着各地域文化族群的集合记忆及身份识别特征，景观既是人文的，也是科学的；既是一部人类文化史，也是一部人类认识自然的科学史，是人类社会和国家民族宝贵的文化遗产。历史不是凝固的，需要演进发展，但不是断裂。很多时候我们现在正在改变的环境、创造的"美丽"、诠释的价值，与它们的历史遗产价值以及其对象已失

去了联系。面对历史的“美丽”，我们既缺乏欣赏能力也弱于继承，是有“审美障碍”的一代，我们已经回不到历史的长河之中，也缺乏传承惠泽未来的能力。今天的中国景观，在全球化的浪潮中，带着不确定的文化漂泊感，正在失去了真正的、本土的“中国式美丽”，中国尚未找回景观的文化自信。

因此，风景园林学科想要为“美丽中国”、“生态文明”做贡献，首先需要具备判断“美丽”的环境价值观，从人与自然的根本关系上认识人类发展的可持续性，在中国历史及社会各族群的传统智慧的继承上，引领全社会对“美丽”环境事物的对象和深度的认知，提高发现“美丽”、阅读“美丽”的能力，持续地维护和创造“美丽”。这种能力的培养，需要我们坚持长期的深度哲学思考，需要向多学科的知识学习，需要向每一个文化族群学习，切实落实环境伦理、社会公平。景观的保护、营造及其创作，是为了解说、展示 “美丽”的内涵，创造体验“美丽”、沉浸“美丽”的场所。保护和实现人与自然的共同“美丽”、诗意栖居，是每一个中国风景园林师的梦想，也是全人类的理想。

we are creating, the value we are interpreting, is disconnected from its historical context. We do not have the knowledge of history to appreciate historical beauty, nor can we inherit such historical legacy. We cannot find the way back home and feel a sense of inability to move into the future without historical power. Today's Chinese landscape, in the wave of globalization and with a sense of uncertainty of its own cultural identity, is losing its authentic Chinese beauty. China has not yet regained its cultural confidence and been able to express this in its new landscape.

Therefore, if the discipline of landscape architecture intends to contribute to Beautiful China and ecological civilization, it first needs a new view of value to judge beauty with environmental concerns, to understand sustainability from the rooted human–nature relationship. The discipline should lead society to identify the "beautiful" objects and understand the profoundness of "beauty," to improve our ability to discover beauty, to read beauty, and to continuously maintain and create beauty. The education and cultivation of these abilities requires us to adhere to long-term deep philosophical thinking, to learn from historical wisdom, from multidisciplinary knowledge, from each cultural group, and to implement environmental ethics and social equity. The protection and the creation of landscape is a way to understand, interpret, and display the meaning of the beauty of life, to create beautiful places to experience beauty. Protecting and creating the common beauty of human and nature poetically inhabiting the earth is a dream of every Chinese, and an ideal of all humankind.

1. Naess A., "The Shallow and the Deep, Long-Range Ecology Movement," *Inquiry* 16 (1973): 95–100.

格林豪泰酒店

SONY

# Beautiful China: Heaven, Earth, and Humanity

## 美丽中国人居风景园林观及其现代性转变

**刘滨谊 | LIU Binyi**

Professor and former Chair, Department of Landscape Studies, Tongji University. Liu was awarded the first PhD in landscape architecture in China, and has completed post-doctoral studies at Virginia Tech in the United States. He has published 15 books and 430 academic papers, and has participated in over 30 scientific research projects and 200 landscape design and planning projects. His research interests include human settlement and environment studies, urban and rural green space system planning, and landscape microclimate adaptability design.

同济大学教授、博导、风景园林科学研究所所长。中国第一位风景园林学博士，美国佛吉尼亚理工及州立大学景观环境规划与GIS应用博士后，同济大学建筑与城市规划学院景观学系首任系主任。他从事风景园林学科专业35年，出版著作15部，发表期刊会议学术论文430多篇，主持完成国家、省部级科研30余项，景观设计规划、绿地系统规划、旅游策划规划等实践项目200多项。研究方向：风景园林分析评价理论与方法、城乡绿地系统规划、风景园林小气候适应性设计。

Chinese people's living environment is considered as the three-dimensional natural *shanshui* (landscape of mountain and water), encapsulating a traditional Chinese aesthetic appreciation of the connection between heaven (the universe) and earth. Different from the scenery of the ancient Greek theater and the pictorial landscape that originated with 17th-century Dutch painters, the concept of Chinese *fengjing* (landscape) is derived from two interdependent aspects of *feng* (wind) and *jing* (shadow). From the Pamir and Kunlun mountain ranges (the ancestors of Chinese mountains), Baoji (the birthplace of the Zhou Dynasty) to Yuncheng in Shanxi Province, and further to the countryside and wilderness, the landscape practice of taking *fengjing* as the intermediary, *shanshui* as the origin, and the beauty of human settlements as the goal, establishes a trinity of heaven, earth, and humanity in harmony. This trinity is the fundamental nexus of Beautiful China and of landscape architecture.

The Taoist belief in the harmony of heaven, earth, and humanity, and settlements formed according to the principles of *shanshui* has underpinned 5,000 years of Chinese agricultural civilization. The image of "blue water and green mountain" is a spiritual and practical sense of place that passes from generation to generation. This goal to create an ideal settlement has also become the core of landscape architecture in China. Unfortunately, in the past 100 years, because of modernization and blindly following Western forms of

development, China has lost the ancient glory of creating beautiful human settlements.

Ancient Chinese people studied *feng* and measured shadows to form *jing* and set the dates of the summer and winter solstices. With the further understanding of *feng* and *jing*, a complete cosmological calendar was developed and people started to appreciate *fengjing* as the key to a harmonious society. Two thousand years ago, landscape aesthetics and gardening practices started to be treated as an art. With the concept of *fengjing*, and the research and practice of gardening, *feng tu* (local customs and culture), *feng shui* (traditional Chinese geomancy), and *feng wu* (local sights and cultural architecture), Chinese landscape architecture was born and integrated with the development of human settlements. Over time the exploration of the heaven–earth–human trinity has related to three different but connected themes: first, the sufficiency of survival; second, the prosperity of the nation and peace of the people; and finally, the poetry of dwelling. Today's Beautiful China is just the modern reoccurrence of the "*fengjing* world."

中国人生存发展的环境是立体的自然山水，自然山水孕育了中国人的人居环境的"山水美感"和"立体的"的世界观，把天（宇宙）、地（地球）联系在一起来感受。既不同于源自古希腊古罗马剧场之景的"风景"，也有别于17世纪启自荷兰画家眼中、后经多学科扩展的"景观"，中国"风景"观念源起于"风"和"景"两个相对独立、后为一体的概念。从帕米尔高原、昆仑山（中国祖山）、陕西宝鸡（周朝的发祥地）到山西运城，再到乡村旷野，以"风景"为媒、以自然山水为源、以追求人居美为目标的实践最终奠定了中国人"天地人+和"的"三位一体"与"三位一求"的世界发展观。"天-地-人"三元一体的世界观也是美丽中国与中国现代景观实践的理念核心 。

"道法自然"，"天地人和"，"山水人居"，始终是美丽中国人居的理想，伴随着华夏子孙成功地走过了5千年的人居农耕文明，"绿水青山观"已成为中国人居理想的基因而世代相传、家喻户晓，以人居美为核心的风景园林则成为了理想人居的化身。然而，在近代一百多年工业文明的人居演进中，中国人的美丽人居环境与世界观却失去了昔日的辉煌，缺少了与古为新和与时俱进的两大文明间的传承与转变，不接中国人居地气的"西风东进”和数典忘祖的“三风渐失”加剧了中国当代人居风景园林的问题恶化。

中国的风景园林观源自中国人居实践，古人研究“风”与“景”，识“风”辨气候，定24节气；“立杆测影”成“景”（发光体、被照体、影），定夏至、冬至。随着对“风”“景”自然的不断探索和实践，中国人进而发现“景风至而天下和”之社会运行规律。2000年前，中国人开始风景游赏与造园实践。以风、景、风景为起点，及至造园、风土、风水、风物的研究与实践，中国的风景园林从源头就与中国人居发展融为一体，在大自然中探求“天-地-人”三元一体的生存、和谐、仙境的理想人居之路和综合研究方法，经历了（1）满足生存、（2）国泰民安、（3）诗意栖居三个阶段。美丽中国正是数千年来“风景天下”观的现代重现。

经过数千年实践的积累，建基于三元论的哲学观不仅具有共生共享和谐的优势，而且可以解决定义西方美学的二元论中对立、分解、分析而缺乏综合环境观所导致的冲突，在后工业文明时代正在日益显示出其现代的生命力。基于中国现代发展中遇到的人口增长与环境恶化等问题，基于三元论的中国风景园林需要在这个时代表达出他新的活力。围绕中国风景园林的现代性，同济大学风景园林在近70年的学科建设、专业教育、科研实践中，开展了全方位、持续性、体系化的探索与发展。

“与古为新”，“与时俱进”，“前瞻超越”，以冯纪忠这三方面的中国风景园林现代性思想精髓为基石，围绕中国风景园林的现代性及其转变，同济大学风景园林系与作者团队也已探索多年，初步构建了基于中国风景观与现代需求的风景园林学科和人居环境科学的三元理论体系。从园林走向风景园林，从风景园林走向人居风景园林，情理交融，主客互动，三元一体，耦合互动，等等，美丽中国风景园林的现代性转变已成势在必行、水到渠成之势。

自新中国建国以来，中国风景园林的现代性的转变已经开始，改革开放的40年更加速了这一转变。面对美丽中国建设，深入认识中国风景园林优秀的传统价值，跳出局限着我们的“小园林”观念思维，走向后工业文明阶段性的现代性转变，这既是实现建设美丽中国的需要，也是中国风景园林的希望之路。

The Chinese trinity of the harmony of heaven, earth, and humanity is a more complete worldview than the dualism that has characterized Western aesthetics (and which has also resulted in a misinterpretation of Taoist philosophy as dualistic between heaven and earth). China was the first country to be confronted with and learn from the problems of human settlements, such as limited resources, environmental deterioration, population growth, social inequality, and political instability. The question now is how to express the unity of heaven, earth, and humanity in the context of post-industrial civilization. This is something we have been working on for the last 70 years at Tongji University's landscape architecture program.

Based on the foundation of Feng Jizhong's theory of landscape architectural modernity, at Tongji we have preliminarily formed a theory of landscape architecture and human settlement centered on the trinity of heaven, earth, and humanity, and systematically developed design methods that manifest a Chinese *fengjing* worldview and meet the demands of contemporary society. The transition to the next level of human settlement provides a significant opportunity for the future of landscape architecture in contemporary China. From gardening to landscape architecture and from landscape architecture to planning human settlements, Beautiful China is a an idea that pursues harmony between art and science, between subjectivity and objectivity, and unifies the two.

Since the founding of the People's Republic of China, the development of Chinese landscape architecture as a profession and academic discipline has accelerated during the last 40 years of China's economic and cultural reforms. With an in-depth understanding of the value of traditional Chinese landscapes, the Beautiful China policy is an effort to manage the forces of modernity; therein lies a path of hope for Chinese landscape architecture.

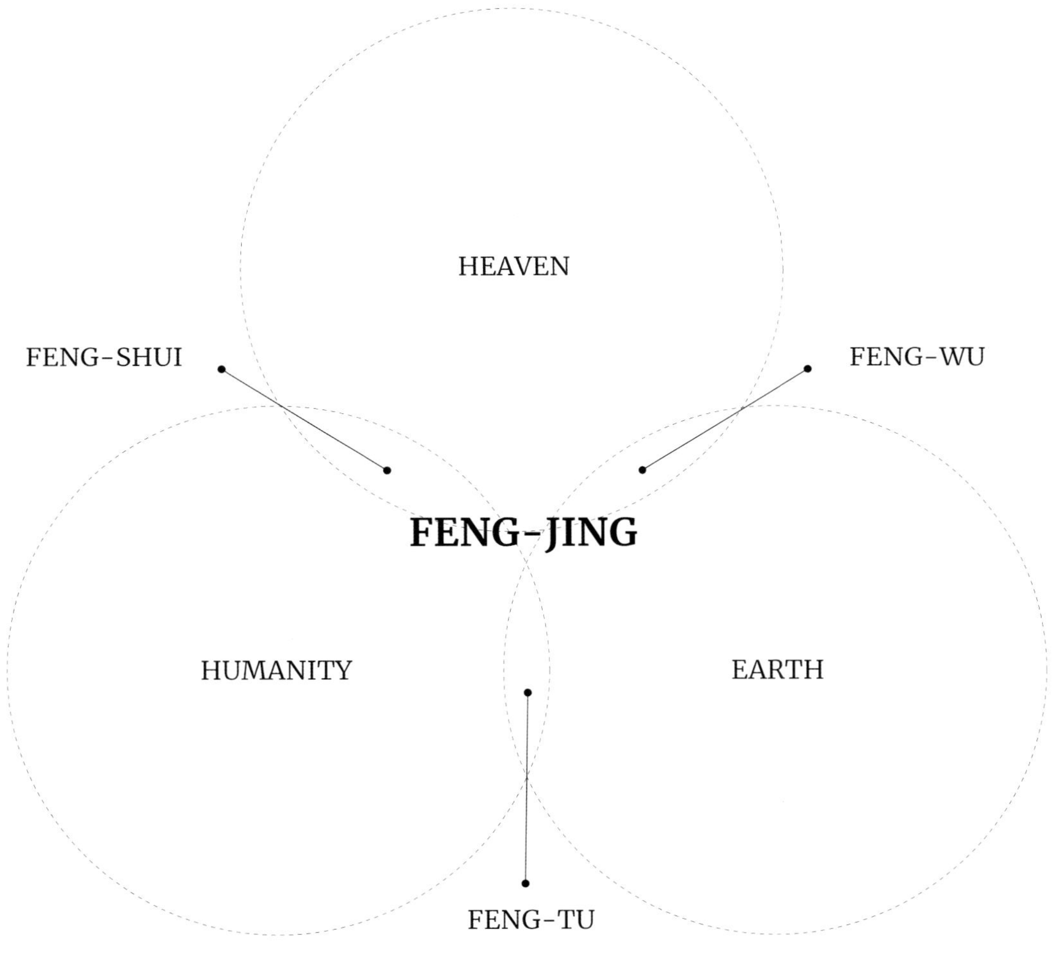

HEAVEN

FENG-SHUI

FENG-WU

**FENG-JING**

HUMANITY

EARTH

FENG-TU

# Landscape and Human Settlement
## 山水与人居

王向荣 | WANG Xiangrong

Dean, School of Landscape Architecture, Beijing Forestry University, and principal of Atelier DYJG. Wang is Vice President of the Chinese Society of Landscape Architecture, Chief Editor of *Landscape Architecture Journal China*, and Deputy Chief Editor of *Chinese Landscape Architecture*. His work has received numerous awards, including honors from the American Society of Landscape Architects, the British Association of Landscape Industries, the International Federation of Landscape Architects Asia-Pacific Region, and the Chinese Society of Landscape Architecture.

北京林业大学园林学院院长。中国风景园林学会常务理事。《风景园林》主编、《中国园林》副主编。设计作品2次获得美国风景园林师协会（ASLA）规划类优秀奖，6次获得英国国家景观奖(BALI)，5次获得国际风景园林师联合会亚太区（IFLA APR）规划设计优秀奖，获中国风景园林学会优秀规划设计一等奖2次。

There are two painting scrolls that enjoy the highest reputation in Chinese history. The first is *The Vast Land* by Wang Ximeng. The painting illustrates vast rivers shrouded in fog, high mountains and hills in folds, and winding paths and streams, interspersed with the architecture of human settlement. With the mountain ranges or waterfronts as the background, the buildings conform to the terrain in sensuous proportions. The painting depicts a beautiful landscape that can be inhabited by humans.

The other painting is the *Riverside Scene at Qingming Festival* by Zhang Zeduan, depicting the canal landscape and commoners' life of the capital city Bianliang during the Northern Song Dynasty. The painting centers on the Bianhe River that flows from the suburb to downtown. It highlights the busy water transportation showing the comprehensive functions of human livelihood, production, and ecology. It is the canal that brought prosperity and vitality to the capital and that nourished the splendid culture of Bianliang.

The content and environment depicted in these two paintings of the Song Dynasty vary greatly from each other. The former elaborates natural landscape and rural settlements while the latter represents the ancient waterside city. Nevertheless, both paintings express the intimate relationship between landscape and human settlement. They also reflect the lifestyle and ideal settlement of the Chinese people.

Chinese people relied on farming to survive when this piece of land was first settled, and China has sustained its splendid civilization for thousands of years on the basis of agriculture. However, China's natural environment does not favor agricultural development in most areas: the annual rainfall distribution does not match the seasonal moisture demands of crop growth. In other words, if the farmland relied only on natural precipitation, the crop production would be unreliable or even catastrophic.

Fortunately, the contiguous mountains feature numerous rivers providing superb conditions for water conservancy. Chinese strived to build various water conservancy works in very early times, utilizing natural water to irrigate croplands and facilitate transportation between different regions, developing, over time, a nationwide artificial-natural water system. This water network supports agricultural production enabling China to maintain a large population with limited acreage of arable land. It also works as an environmental support system, providing for times of drought and weakening flood intensity, improving rural and urban resilience.

Traditional Chinese agriculture is labor-intensive with the farmland maintained through laborious care, so villages are generally sited in accessible distance to farmland. The water conservancy facilities supporting agricultural production therefore also provide the infrastructure to support the life of the villagers. *The Vast Land* by Wang Ximeng elaborates the natural water-linked villages and settlements in foothills and piedmonts. As a highly generalized representation of rural settlement, the painting reflects the unique landscape-fused human settlement of rural area in China.

Villages are often the embryos of cities in human history. The land consolidation in agricultural civilization gradually transforms into the basic norms of urban planning. Urban growth is sustained through the constructed hydrological system of lakes, canals, and irrigation channels. *Riverside Scene at Qingming Festival* demonstrates amply the prosperity and vitality brought by an artificial canal to the city. It can be seen from the painting that the canal connects the quiet countryside with the bustling downtown area.

中国历史上有两幅最著名的绘画长卷。其一是王希孟的“千里江山图”。画面上江水烟波浩渺，崇山峻岭层峦叠嶂，山中小径曲折盘旋，溪流飞瀑溅泻，山间点缀着农舍、村落、寺观、亭台水榭、磨坊和大小桥梁，建筑群无论是背山还是滨水，都随山就势，错落有致。画面描绘的是可居宜居的秀丽江山。

另一幅是张择端的“清明上河图”，这幅长卷描绘了北宋都城汴京的运河风景和市井风俗。画面以汴河为中心，从郊外逐渐过渡到城市。从中我们可以看出，汴河不仅承担着都城繁忙的水上运输，还具有各种综合复杂的生产、生活和生态功能。运河为汴京带去繁荣与活力，也滋养了汴京灿烂的文化。

这两幅宋画表达的内容及环境完全不同，前者描绘的是自然山水与乡村聚落；后者展现的是城水相融的古代城市，但两者都表达了山水与人居的密切关系，也反映了中国人的生活方式和人居理想。

中国人开始在这片土地上定居，依赖的是农业。中国是一个农业国家，几千年的灿烂文明都是建立在农业基础之上的。但其实，中国的自然条件对于发展农业来说有特别不利的一面，即大部分地区降水的年度分布与农作物生长的需水周期不能吻合。农业生产如果依靠自然降水，不仅不可靠，有可能还是灾难性的。

好在中国连绵不断的山脉孕育了数不清的河流，这为发展水利提供了优越的条件。中国人很早就开始建造各种水利设施，力求改造自然水环境，控制自然水文，为农业生产提供灌溉用水，也为不同地区之间的交通运输提供便利，于是在国土上逐渐形成了人工与自然结合的规模宏大的水系网络。这张水网支撑了农业生产，保证了中国在耕地有限的情况下养育了大量的人口；它也是环境支撑系统，减少了水害的压力，减弱了水害的强度，使得乡村和城市更具有弹性。

由于中国的传统农业是一种劳动密集型农业，农田需要通过大量的劳作进行照料和维护，因此在一定范围的农田中必须有村落，两者相互依存，缺一不可。建造村落整理土地的方式与农地的整理方式是一致的，村落与农地的规划是一体的，支撑农业生产的水利设施也是支撑村民生活的基础设施。每个地区的农业与聚落相对稳

《千里江山图》王希孟
*The Vast Land* by Wang Ximeng

定，世代沿袭，经过漫长的时间积累，形成了一个个乡村景观单元。王希孟的“千里江山图”描绘的就是自然的河流湖泊串联起的位于山谷和山前地带的乡村与聚落，是高度概括的乡村人居环境。虽说有艺术化和理想化的成分，但反映了中国特有的与山水高度融合的乡村人居环境。

历史上许多城市的胚胎就是村落。农耕文明的土地整理经验，也逐渐转化成古人城市空间营建的基本准则。城市与农业的水环境目标在本质上是一致的，即稳定和可控。各地依据不同的自然条件创造出的农业生产支撑系统，如陂塘、运河、灌渠等，实际上也是城市的环境支撑系统。城市的功能和结构与这一系统密切相关。“清明上河图”就充分表现了一条人工运河为城市带来的繁荣和活力。从画面上看，这条运河将恬静的乡村与繁华的都城联系了起来；而在画面之外，这条运河与城市内外大大小小的人工与自然河湖一同构成了完整的水网，联系了帝国的广大疆域，沟通了不同地区的交通，为农田提供了灌溉，为城市提供了弹性的水的调蓄。

在漫长的农业社会，依靠不断积累的经验，我们的祖先一直在不同的地区，针对不同的自然条件，进行相应的水利建设、耕地拓展、土壤改良和家园营建，创造了整体的山水人居环境。这一过程并非是一帆风顺的，在各种历史记载中有不少失败的案例，也有一些历史上的开发和建设带来了环境的退化，如黄河中游丘陵山区的森林砍伐和农业垦殖是造成今天这些地区生态环境脆弱的主要原因。但是，仍然有大量成功的建设成果留存至今，如建造于两千年前的都江堰和灵渠，今天仍在发挥着当初的作用。还有许多历史悠久的城市，在古代修建了完善的陂塘河渠系统，虽然在今天这些系统的灌

What is not seen is that the canal, as part of an integrated water network linking numerous artificial and natural rivers and lakes in and out of the capital city, extended to the vast territory, connecting and sustaining the whole empire.

In China’s long agricultural history, ancestors in different regions of the territory have accumulated and passed on their experiences of utilizing the natural conditions for construction of water conservancy systems, expanding arable land, and improving soils. These experiences include both successes and failures. For example, deforestation and agricultural cultivation in the hilly area of the middle reaches of the Yellow River have resulted in environmental degradation and the current fragile ecological condition in these areas. On the other hand, the Dujiangyan Irrigation System and Lingqu Canal, which were both built two thousand years ago, are still functioning and contributing to the agricultural and environmental successes of their regions. Many historic cities—such as Hangzhou, Fuzhou, Huizhou, and Ningbo—also built complete artificial lake systems in ancient times, and although their roles in irrigation, water supply, and shipping have now weakened or disappeared, they still hold significant practical and cultural value in ecological conservation, recreation, and tourism. They are authentic models of sustainability.

Today, in the face of rapidly evolving human settlement, as well as the increasingly prominent problems of environmental pollution, ecosystem fragmentation, and cultural discontinuity we must ask whether current sustainability theory serves the

《清明上河图》 张择端
*Riverside Scene at Qingming Festival* by Zhang Zeduan

land better than the successful practices of our ancestors. How best can the unique landscapes illustrated in *The Vast Land* and *Riverside Scene at Qingming Festival* be sustained?

溉、供水和航运功能已经弱化或消失了，但却承载着更多的生态、游憩、文化和风景的价值，如杭州西湖、济南大明湖、福州西湖、宁波东钱湖和惠州西湖等等。难以想象世界上还有哪些人工设施具有如此强大的生命力，能够历经上千年的环境与社会的变化，依然为人们提供服务。它们堪称可持续的典范。

今天，面对正在迅速改变的传统人居环境，面对愈加突出的环境污染、生态系统破碎、文化延续断裂等问题，我们不得不发出疑问：近40年的土地利用方式和建设途径是否能够很好地适合这片土地？各种可持续的理论是否真的比祖先留给我们的成功经验更加高明？已经延续了几千年的中国特有的山水人居是否还能持续？

政策景觀

# 政策景观
# The Policy Landscape

夺取新时代中

色社会主义伟大胜利
东
06
Hisens
东站欢迎您

# Representations of Beautiful China
# 图像化“美丽中国”

**赵纪军 | ZHAO Jijun**

Professor, School of Architecture and Urban Planning, Huazhong University of Science and Technology. Zhao holds a PhD from the University of Sheffield and is a member of the Theory and History Committee and the Cultural Landscape Committee of the Chinese Society of Landscape Architecture. He is author of *Chinese Modern Landscape Architecture: A Historical and Theoretical Study* (2014) and *Chinese Pavilion* (2019).

英国谢菲尔德大学风景园林博士，现为华中科技大学建筑与城市规划学院教授，博士生导师，中国风景园林学会理论历史专业委员会委员、中国风景园林学会文化景观专业委员会委员。主要从事风景园林历史与理论领域的研究，著有《中国现代园林：历史与理论研究》以及《亭引》。

The call for a Beautiful China was issued at the 18th National Congress of the Chinese Communist Party (CCP) in November 2012, but the national pursuit of beauty certainly did not just come after the new millennium. In fact, it had been part of the ideal of the gardening movement initiated by Chairman Mao Zedong in August 1958 for the development of socialist China.

> “We should turn all the lands of our country green and make it a garden, so that it will be beautiful everywhere, and the natural condition will be changed. Trees should be well planted…it is like a garden everywhere. As such, the standard of communism will be fulfilled.”[1]

In Mao’s initiatives, there were several layers of meanings to the concept of beauty. First, the design and creation of a beautiful park or garden showed its relationship with the professional practice of landscape architecture. Second, the basis for being beautiful was “greening,” which demonstrated its relationship with planting or forestry. And third, beauty was related to the natural features of the country. In the Sixth Plenary Session of the Eighth Central Committee of the CCP in 1958, the call for the National Greening and Gardening Movement was issued in the Resolution on Several Issues of the People’s Communes. This call again emphasised planting and visual appreciation of the landscape, carrying forward Chairman Mao’s concept of the “beautiful.”

1958年出版的“特27-林业建设”系列邮票
Stamps depicting “forestry development” issued in 1958

> “According to local conditions, we should try to gradually reduce the cultivated land to about one third in a few years. Some of the land can lie fallow for crop rotation, and plant grass and weeds that can be used as fertilizer. On the other land, we should plant trees, dig lakes and retain water. On the flat grounds, on the mountains and in the water, ornamental plants with vivid colours can be planted so as to put into practice the National Landscaping and Gardening Movement.”[2]

The contemporary concept of Beautiful China is made more important because it is connected to the notion of “ecological civilization,” which means that the pursuit of beauty should be integrated into the whole development process of economic, political, cultural, and social construction. It is also written into the 13th Five-Year Plan (2016–2020), which is the first time that both beauty and ecological issues have become important parts of a Five-Year Plan. The beauty of contemporary China, therefore, not only exists in visual appreciation, but is also relevant to green development, environmental governance,

2012年11月8日，十八大报告提出“美丽中国”理念，但显然并非新千年之后才出现对于“美丽”的追求。追溯历史，我们发现，对于社会主义中国而言，“美丽”这一概念早已蕴含在1958年毛泽东提出的“园林化”号召之中：

“要使我们祖国的山河全部绿化起来，要达到园林化，到处都很美丽，自然面貌得到改变。种树要种好，……到处像公园，做到这样，就达到共产主义的要求[1]。”

关于“美丽”，这段话表达了几层意思：第一，大地因为“园林”和“公园”——所以“美丽”，这显示了与风景园林行业的关系；第二，“美丽”的基础是“绿化”，显示了与植树造林之林业的关系；第三，“美丽”与国土的自然面貌相关，是社会主义、共产主义的价值之一。随后，《关于人民公社若干问题的决议》发出了“大地园林化”的号召：

“应当争取在若干年内，根据地方条件，把现有种农作物的耕地面积逐步缩减到1/3左右，而以其余的一部分土地实行轮休，种牧草、肥田草，另一部分土地植树造林，挖湖蓄水，在平地、山上和水面都可以大种其万紫

1958年出版的"特27-林业建设"系列邮票
Stamps depicting "forestry development" issued in 1958

ecological protection, and the environmental regulatory system. Beautiful China thus comprises various aspects of national development, making it more comprehensive than Chairman Mao's National Landscaping and Gardening Movement. In this era of Beautiful China, the improvement of the quality of people's living environments has become the main goal of the government. In the Mao Zedong era, one of the most important governing philosophies was "to serve the people." When the call for Beautiful China was issued, President Xi Jinping also said that the "people's pursuit for a good and beautiful life is the goal for us to strive for."

So what does Beautiful China mean for the people, and how do people perceive and understand this concept? One lens through which to evaluate this is through propaganda in the form of government-issued postage stamps. Although there was no single stamp representing the National Landscaping and Gardening Movement, a series of stamps depicting "forestry development" was issued in 1958. These emphasized tree planting as the basis for the construction of China as a "beautiful garden." Accordingly, in the early 1950s, tree planting became a national priority, and a common slogan was "green first, beautification second." In the editorial of the *People's Daily* on March 9, 1959, the declared goal of the National Landscaping and Gardening Movement was to "Green the Motherland."[3]

Following the policy declaration in 2012, stamps depicting Beautiful China were issued in 2013. The series of stamps include images of Xiapu Beach, the natural reserves of Zhangjiajie Tianzi Mountain, Panjin Red Beach, the tropical islands of Sansha, the agricultural landscapes of Longsheng Rice Terrace, and the stack fields of Xinghua. In May 2016, a second series consisting of four more stamps was issued depicting the national forest park "Snow County of Mudanjiang," the national geological park "Ten-Thousand-Peak Forest of Xingyi," the natural reserve "Sha Lake of Shizui Mountain," and the national wetland park "Hangzhou Xixi Wetland." Many of these sites are major tourist attractions, which are meant to integrate ecological, social, and economic values and benefits. The stamps make it clear that the visual spectacle of the natural landscape is the dominant image

千红的观赏植物，实行大地园林化[2]。”在此，一是仍然强调绿化植树，二是强调视觉品质，延续了“美丽”的内涵。

新千年之初提出的“美丽中国”理念，把生态文明建设放在突出地位，融入经济建设、政治建设、文化建设、社会建设各方面和全过程，并被纳入“十三五”规划（2016–2020），这也是首次将“美丽”及“生态”问题纳入五年计划。在此，“美丽”不仅仅在于视觉的愉悦，更与绿色发展、环境治理、生态保护、监管体制相关，强调人与自然之间的和谐关系，囊括了国家建设发展各个方面的、更为丰富、综合的内容。从“大地园林化”到“美丽中国”，从根本上说，都是为了提升人居环境的品质，增进社会大众的福祉。毛泽东时代最为重要的执政理念之一便是“为人民服务”；“美丽中国”提出之时，习近平总书记也说：“人民对美好生活的向往，就是我们的奋斗目标。”

那么从“大地园林化”到“美丽中国”的理念更新，对于人民大众而言，意味着什么？人民大众的认知和理解如何？对于这个问题可以通过公众媒体发布的宣传图像加以认识，因其源于公众，又面向公众。本文以公开发行的邮票为切入点，探讨这一问题。对于“大地园林化”并没有相应邮票的图像呈现，但1958年出版的“特27-林业建设”系列邮票可借以说明当时人们对于“大地园林化”的理解。如前述，“美丽”的“园林”以“绿化”植树为基础，因此在建国后“百废待兴”的政治、社会、经济背景下，“绿化”植树成为首要的工作，即“先绿化，后美化”，甚至《人民日报》在1959年3月9日的社论中，称大地园林化“是我国的造林事业的远大的目标，是绿化祖国的最高标准[3]”。从邮票图像的内容来看，主要体现为通过群众运动的植树造林实践，其“美丽”的愿景是建设一个拥有“绿色”国土的现代国家。

“美丽中国”理念提出的次年，即2013年5月，发行了第一套“美丽中国”邮票，一共6枚，包括被誉为“中国最美丽滩涂”的“霞浦滩涂”、自然保护区“张家界天子山”和“盘锦红海滩”、热带海岛“三沙七连屿”、农耕景观“龙胜梯田”和“兴化垛田”。2016年5月，发行了第二套、共4枚邮票，包括国家森林公园“牡丹江雪乡”、国家地质公园“兴义万峰林”、自然保护区“石嘴山沙湖”、国家湿地公园“杭州西溪湿地”。这些地点很多同时还是4A或5A级旅游景区，整合了生态效益、社会效益和经济效益。这些图像对于现实图景的再现，能够反映“美丽中国”理念中的诸多风景园林价值，其中可称作“美丽”的特质包括：基于视觉的大地风景奇观、城市与区域的和谐共存关系、国土的幅员辽阔和地大物博、本土的文化与历史、保存良好的自然资源、具有生物多样性的生境等。

有关“大地园林化”的“林业建设”系列邮票与“美丽中国”系列邮票，都反映了国土大地营造及其变迁的现实与理想，也都有着一方面改造、改善自然环境，另一方面保护自然资源的理念。但前者内容相对单一，主要关于全民“植树”及其一般性成果；后者内容相对丰富，在新的时代条件下，其体现的政治、社会、生态等价值也更为具体而多样。毛泽东时代的“大地园林化”愿景，是将整个中国建设成为一个“大公园”“大花园”[4]，然而其实践存在林业建设与风景园林实践的分野。前者——如前述——主要在于植树造林，是大众的一般认知与理解；后者主要局限于城市绿化和公园的建设，而没有体现“大地园林化”对改善国土面貌的高标准的展望。因而，风景园林实践的价值关切与“大地园林化”的视野有所偏差，风景园林行业在“大地园林化”实践中的角色则有其模糊性和不确定性。

与此不同，上述大众认知中的“美丽中国”内容，有不少已是如今风景园林行业实践的重要组成部分，如自然保护区、湿地公园等，因而风景园林实践的价值关切与“美丽中国”的视野有一致性。在“美丽中国”的愿景下，风景园林行业实践对于“美丽”的呈现、对于增进社会大众的福祉，有着更为显性而切实的作用。可见，从“大地园林化”到“美丽中国”，“美丽”正在变成现实，中国的大地风景正发生着诸多有益的改变。然而，也应当看到，“美丽中国”的提出呼吁“生态文明”，也反衬了环境问题的严峻性，在这一意义上，风景园林行业也当有所为。

of beauty. This image of beauty is more than just scenery, it implies a harmony between nature and culture.

Both the 1958 and 2013–2016 sets of stamps champion the improvement of the landscape, but the National Landscaping and Gardening Movement images were somewhat simpler in content. They expressed tree planting through mass mobilization, while the contemporary Beautiful China stamps are symbolic of political, social, and ecological values in the new era. The ideal of the National Landscaping and Gardening Movement in the Mao era was to turn the whole of China into an enormous park or garden.[4] But in practice, there is a divergence between forestry and landscape architecture. The former, which is more widely understood and accepted by the public, concerns large-scale tree planting whereas the latter concerns urban green space and park development, which lacks the holistic vision of improving the whole nation. This divergence has caused ambiguity and uncertainty both within the National Landscaping and Gardening Movement and the modern landscape architecture discipline in China.

However, the practical conception of Beautiful China—as understood by the general public and as shown in the stamps—actually corresponds quite closely with aspects of current landscape architectural professional practice. For example, Chinese landscape architects are working on scenic values in national parks and the conservation of protected areas, as well as the creation of wetlands and other landscapes to support biodiversity. Thus, it can be seen that landscape architectural values are consistent with the vision of Beautiful China and the role of the landscape architectural discipline in helping to create Beautiful China is relatively clear. But it is also important to note that the current call for an ecological civilization acknowledges the existence of serious environmental problems that go well beyond the scenery depicted on the stamps. In this regard, it seems there is considerable scope for the landscape architectural discipline to extend its reach and make an impact.

1. Mao Zedong, "We Should Turn All the Lands of Our Country Green" (August 1958), http://www.forestry.gov.cn/ZhuantiAction.do?dispatch=content&id=266164&name=ly60.
2. "Resolution on Several Issues of the People's Communes (Approved in the Sixth Plenary Session of the Eighth Central Committee of the CCP)," *People's Daily* (December 19, 1958).
3. "Accelerate the Speed of Greening and Improve the Quality of Afforestation," *People's Daily* (March 9, 1959).
4. Zhao J., "A Historical Survey of the National Landscaping and Gardening Movement," *Chinese Landscape Architecture* 26, no. 10 (2010): 56–60.

《美丽中国》普通邮票第一组，五图：龙胜梯田（1.50元）

2016年出版的第二套"美丽中国"系列邮票
Stamps depicting "Beautiful China" issued in 2016

# Beyond Beauty
# 超越美丽

**杨锐 | YANG Rui**

Chair, Department of Landscape Architecture, School of Architecture, Tsinghua University, and founder and dean of the National Park Research Institute of Tsinghua University. As the group leader of experts, Yang led the drafting of China's first Five-Year Plan for the Conservation of Cultural and Natural Heritage. Currently, he serves as an expert consultant to the Ministry of Education, the National Development and Reform Commission, the National Forestry and Grass Bureau, the Ministry of Housing and Construction, and the Ministry of Culture and Tourism.

清华大学建筑学院景观学系联合创始人、系主任，清华大学国家公园研究院院长。作为专家组组长，主持起草了中国第一部文化与自然遗产保护五年规划纲要，主持完成了十多个中国国家公园和自然保护地总体规划。目前应邀担任教育部、国家发改委、国家林草局、住建部、文旅部等多个政府部门的专家咨询工作。

I have been at Tsinghua University since 1984 – first, as an undergraduate and master's student, and then as a doctoral candidate and teacher. Over this time, my academic focus has shifted from construction to protection, from cities to national parks and protected areas. For more than 20 years, I have been involved in many important practical works of large-scale landscape protection, such as the Northwest Yunnan National Park and Protected Area System, the Qinba Mountain National Park and Protected Area System, the Inner Mongolia Natural Conservation System Strategy Research, and relevant planning work for natural heritage sites such as Mount Taishan, Mount Huangshan, Meili Snow Mountain, Jiuzhaigou Valley, Mount Wutai, Mount Wuyi, Mount Huashan, Jianfengling Mountain Forest Park, Longmenshan Mountain, the Wudalianchi, and Sanjiangyuan. In 2003, Professor Laurie Olin and I founded the Department of Landscape Architecture of the School of Architecture of Tsinghua University. Then, I participated in the declaration of the first-level discipline (of landscape architecture) and was the president of the Chinese Teaching Guidance Committee of Landscape Architecture Education and the Committee of Theory and History of the Chinese Society of Landscape Architecture.

Over these years in practice and teaching, I have been thinking about the question, "What kind of landscape architecture discipline does China

need in the early 21st century?" In 2014, I published an essay titled "*Jing-Qi-Di*: A Framework of Chinese Landscape Architecture," attempting to construct the conceptual framework of landscape architecture with 11 Chinese characters, Tao (道), Values (德), Principles (理), Technologies (术), Functions (用), Mechanisms (制), Images (相), Meanings (意), Environment (境), Land (地), and People (其). This was a preliminary answer to the above question. Today, thanks to the Penn-China Design Dialogues, I can confidently answer this question about the survival, destiny, and prospects of Chinese landscape architecture in a more-specific and bold way. My suggestion is to reshape 21st-century Chinese landscape architecture with the creation of *di-jing* (地境).

The *di-jing* is a meta-concept of landscape architecture formed by the combination of "natural environment," "artistic environment," and "built environment," and contained in national land and territory. A simple formula can express it clearly: *di-jing* = national land and territory +

我从1984年开始进入清华大学学习，先后获得建筑学学士、城市规划和设计硕士，以及风景园林规划设计方向的博士学位。1991年开始在清华大学建筑学院城市规划系工作。从1990年代中期开始，我的注意力从建设转向保护，从城市转向国家公园和自然保护地。20多年来有意识地承担了很多大尺度风景保护的重要实践工作，例如滇西北国家公园和保护地体系、秦巴山脉国家公园和自然保护地体系规划研究、内蒙古自然保护体系战略研究，以及泰山、黄山、梅里雪山、九寨沟、五台山、武夷山、华山、尖峰岭、龙门山、五大连池、三江源等自然保护地的相关规划工作。2003年与Laurie Olin教授一起创办清华大学建筑学院景观学系，其后又深度参与了一级学科的申报，负责（中国）高等学校风景园林学教学指导委员会以及中国风景园林学会理论和历史专业委员会的工作。

在上述工程实践和教育实践中，我一直在思考一个问题"21世纪初中国需要怎样的风景园林学?"。以此为题，一边思考，一边多次做过相关的学术报告。2014年发表了论文《论"境"与"境其地"》，试图以道、德、理、术、用、制、象、意、境、其、地等11个汉字构建风景园林学的概念框架。这算得上是对上述问题较为系统全面的初步回答。今天，我想利用宾大中国论坛这个机会，借用“美丽中国”这个主题，更有针对性、更明确、也更大胆地回答这个关系到中国风景园林学科生存、命运和前景的问题。我的建议是：以地境营造为硬核重塑21世纪中国风景园林学！

所谓“地境”，是以国土空间为容器，化合“生境”、“意境”和“建成环境”所形成的风景园林学元概念！用一个简单公式来表达：地境=国土空间+自然属性+人类属性（人类活动、人工设施、审美价值），或者用复杂一些的公式：地境=国土空间+自然生态属性+人类活动属性+人工设施属性+审美价值；用一句话来表达，地境是拥有自然生态、人类活动、人工设施等属性，并同时具有审美价值的特定国土空间。营造是指保护、规划、设计、建设、维护、管理等专业手段。保护、维护、管理大体属于“营”的范畴；规划、设计、建设大体属于“造”的范畴。

为什么建议21世纪以地境营造为硬核重塑中国风景园林学？第一，土地或者说国土空间是风景园林学研究和实践的主体对象，这一点很多极具前瞻性的前辈都曾指出过。例如汪菊渊先生的“大地景物规划”、孙筱翔先生的“地球表层规划”和吴良镛先生的“地景学”。大家可以看到三者的共同点就是“地”。可惜的是，这三位中国风景园林学权威的超前认识并没有变成风景园林学界的主流认知。第二，生态文明、美丽、美好生活已经成为中国的国家发展目标，而国土空间规划改革、自然资源部和国家公园管理局的成立都是服务于这些目标的工具。在国土空间规划尚未成型之际，风景园林学有潜力也有机会，发挥自己的“整合性（联结、综合、整体）和落地性”优势，明确学科的研究和实践对象是“具有自然生态、人类活动和人工设施等三重属性及审美价值的国土空间”，简而言之即“地境”。亮出这个姿态并以此为硬核建设自己的学术概念体系以及方法技术体系，风景园林学就有可能成为生态文明和美丽中国建设的核心学科；成为人类世和生态生代的核心学科。否则风景园林学不仅面临进一步边缘化的危险，甚至学科生存和基本发展都会成为一个严峻的问题。

如何以地境营造为硬核重塑中国风景园林学？第一要分析时代需求。在我们现在所处的时代，一定要在风景园林学中强调保护和规划的地位。第二，要全面、系

natural attributes + human attributes (human activities, constructed facilities, aesthetic values). A more complex formula could also express it well: *di-jing* = national land and territory + natural ecological attributes + human activity attributes + constructed facility attributes + aesthetic values. “Constructed” here refers to the professional means of protection, planning, design, construction, maintenance, and management of the land. Protection, maintenance, and management generally belong to the category of “managing;” while planning, design, and construction typically fall into the category of “making.”

Why is it recommended to reshape Chinese landscape architecture based on the *di-jing* framework in the 21st century? First, the land or the national territory is the main object of landscape architecture research and practice, which has been pointed out by many forward-looking predecessors. For example, Wang Juyuan’s “Land Scenery Planning,” Sun Xiaoxiang’s “Earthscape Planning,” and Wu Liangyong’s “Earthscape Theory.” Everyone can see that the commonality of the three theories is *di* (land). It is a pity that the prescient insight of these three Chinese landscape architecture authorities has not entered the mainstream cognition of landscape architecture. Second, ecological civilization, beauty, and a better life have become China’s national development goals, and the establishment of the Land and Space Planning Reform, the Ministry of Natural Resources, and the National Park Service are all tools to serve these goals. At the time when national spatial planning for the land has not yet been determined, landscape architecture has the potential and opportunity to clarify a research and practice agenda that brings natural ecology, human activities, artificial infrastructures, and aesthetic values together. In short, this is *di* (land). Showing this attitude and using it as a framework to build its own academic conceptual system and method, landscape architecture may become the core discipline responsible for the creation of ecological civilization and Beautiful China. Otherwise, landscape architecture will not only be marginalized in the future, but its survival and development as a discipline will become a serious problem.

But how can we reshape Chinese landscape architecture based on the creation of *di-jing*? The first step is to analyze the demands of the time. We must emphasize the status of protection and planning in landscape architecture in the era we are living in. Second, it is necessary to comprehensively, systematically, evenly, and deeply study the eight categories of Tao (道), Values (德), Principles (理), Technologies (术), Functions (用), Mechanisms (制), Images (相), Meanings (意), especially to strengthen the study of theory and mechanism. Third, based on the goal of creating *di-jing*, we need to adjust the undergraduate and postgraduate curriculum systems as soon as possible. Fourth, we need to actively participate in national land planning reform, national parks and nature reserve system construction, Beautiful China, and other major national strategies. And finally, we need to maintain the appropriate tension between modernity and Chinese identity.

统、均衡、深化研究道、德、理、术、用、制、象、意八个范畴，尤其要加强学理和机制的研究。第三，以地境营造为目标，尽快调整本科、研究生课程体系。第四，积极参与国土空间规划改革、国家公园和自然保护地体系建设、美丽中国等国家重大战略。第五，保持现代性和中国性之间的适当张力。

# Institutional Construction of Beautiful China
# 美丽中国的制度建设


**张振威 | ZHANG Zhenwei**

Assistant Professor and Associate Dean, School of Architecture and Urban Planning, Beijing University of Civil Engineering and Architecture. Zhang's main research fields are urban and landscape law and policy, landscape ecological planning, and landscape planning and design. He has led or participated in a number of major research projects for the National Nature Science Foundation, the Beijing Municipal Commission of Education, and the National Natural Science Foundation, among others. He has published more than 10 papers in journals including *Urban Planning International*, *Tsinghua Discourses on Rule-of-Law*, *Chinese Landscape Architecture*, and *Landscape Architecture*.

北京建筑大学建筑与城市规划学院，助理教授、副系主任。主要研究方向有城市与景观法律与政策，景观生态规划、景观规划设计。主持国家自然科学基金1项，北京市教委社科重点项目1项，参加国家社科重大、国家自然科学基金5项。在《国际城市规划》、《清华法治论衡》、《中国园林》、《风景园林》等中文核心、CSSCI刊物上发表论文10余篇。


Institutional and legislative change has always been an important factor of promoting the theory and practice of landscape architecture historically. For example, in the second half of the 20th century, the United States formulated a sound environmental legal system with the enactment of laws such as the National Environmental Policy Act (NEPA) and the Coastal Barrier Resources Act. In the 1960s and 1970s NEPA became a milestone in global environmental legislation, stipulating the necessity of consultation with "environmental design" experts and thus augmenting the rise of environmental design schools, particularly in California. Similarly, based on their strong landscape traditions, European countries have also generally constructed national policies and matching institutions to make environmental values a core element in the governance of their lands. In the 21st century this is now enshrined in the European Landscape Convention. The legalization of ecological and environmental matters has introduced a new era for landscape architecture, impacting the discipline from its theories to its institutions.

Following the 18th Chinese Communist Party National Congress in 2012, China has promoted the construction of ecological civilization to the same level as economic construction, political construction, cultural construction, and social construction. This is a historic opportunity for the development of landscape architecture. However, there has not yet been much discussion on

how institution-led construction of ecological civilization will affect Chinese landscape architecture. The central government's promotion of Beautiful China and ecological civilization construction will encourage local people to pay more attention to the natural environment. Both policies will encourage planning and design that is guided by territorial optimization, resource conservation, and environmental protection. This will eliminate some upper-level structural and institutional contradictions hindering the practice of landscape architecture and profoundly change the status, methods and theories, and organization of the profession in China.

The main way to achieve the goals of ecological civilization construction and Beautiful China is through comprehensive institutional provisions. The institutions of territorial spatial planning—which takes its core mission as the rational protection and effective allocation of resources—will coordinate all kinds of spatial planning based on the Plan for Development Priority Zones and finally promote "integration of multiple planning

制度演变是推动风景园林理论与实践发展的重要驱动因子。20世纪后半叶，美国制定了完善的环境法律体系，《国家环境政策法》、《海岸屏障资源法》等多部法律的出台。在被称为"环境时代"的20世纪60–70年代，美国制定了完善的环境法律体系，《国家环境政策法》成为全球环境立法的里程碑。正是因为美国《国家环境政策法》中规定了向"环境设计"专业进行咨询，才导致加州环境设计流派的兴起。生态环境的法制化从理论到制度为风景园林学开辟了新纪元。进入21世纪，基于强大的景观传统，以《欧洲景观公约》为最典型的全球景观法治的范例，欧洲各国普遍建构了以景观为核心的国家政策与关键制度，并使景观上升为国家治理体系的核心要素。

十八大之后，我国将生态文明建设提升到与经济建设、政治建设、文化建设、社会建设同等的五位一体高度，对风景园林学发展而言，是历史性契机。以制度建设为先导的生态文明，对中国风景园林实践会有怎样的影响，尚没有引起广泛的关注和讨论。中央政府所倡导的美丽中国与生态文明建设将鼓励当地居民更重视自然环境的保护。这两项政策也将促进以国土空间优化、资源节约、生态环境保护的良治为导向的规划与设计。同时也将摒除

了生态环境领域形式主义和官僚主义，优化了风景园林实践的软环境，并将深远地影响中国风景园林学科的地位，实践与理论，以及组织结构。

实现生态文明建设和美丽中国的目标的主要途径是全方位的相关制度供给。以空间资源的合理保护和有效配置为核心的国土空间规划制度将以主体功能区规划为基础统筹各类空间性规划，推进“多规合一”。未来的国土空间规划立法，将成为人居环境建设领域的基本法和《城乡规划法》的上位法。风景园林实践有可能参与到从国土空间规划到场地设计的全尺度实践对象当中。生态红线制度旨在构筑以生态安全和生态系统服务为导向的土地利用管制，使风景园林实践建立更为坚固的科学基础以及更为明确的可持续性目标。建立以国家公园为主体的自然保护地体系在保障生物多样性与生态安全的同时，使风景资源回归公益本位，真正保障民众的游憩权益，实现以风景为媒介的社会公正、社会环境伦理、生态旅游与可持续发展观。

生态文明制度建设对学科发展带来机遇，但更重要的是如何把握机遇的挑战。在理论层面，应当开展风景园

systems.” The forthcoming legislation dealing with territorial spatial planning will become the basic law in relation to space planning and site design in China. The “ecological baseline” system aims to establish land-use regulations based on ecological security and ecosystem services, so as to establish a more solid scientific basis for landscape architecture and a clearer goal of sustainability. Establishing a national protected areas system with the national park as the main body will ensure biodiversity and ecological security and, at the same time, relate landscape to national identity and social well-being. This will guarantee the public’s recreational rights, and realize landscape as the medium of social justice and environmental ethics, as well as boost eco-tourism and sustainable development.

The question for landscape architecture in China, then, is how best to grasp the opportunities in both theory and practice that ecological civilization construction presents. In terms of theory, it is necessary to promote interdisciplinary research on landscape architecture, law, institutional economics, and other disciplines. The key issues may include legally defining the profession of landscape architecture in China and establishing a registration and certification system for practitioners. Recognizing how specific laws affect the practice of landscape architecture is also important; for example, the impact of the Prevention and Control of Soil Pollution Act on the green space system. Landscape architects should also engage the legislative process supporting planning and design actions, such as making laws for national parks and protected areas.

In terms of practice, landscape architecture should formally be acknowledged as a leading profession in the construction of ecological civilization and be promoted at the national strategic level. To achieve this, landscape analysis approaches, such as landscape character assessment and landscape quality objectives, should be affirmed as a substantive consideration in all fields of planning and design, from territorial spatial planning to site design, and from environmental impact assessment to the drafting of design guidelines.

Finally, ecological civilization construction is both an opportunity and a challenge for landscape architecture – the competition with other disciplines is increasingly fierce, and the scope of competing disciplines will also be expanded. In addition to planning and design theory, the core theory of landscape architecture shall also include management, sociology, law, economics, and other disciplines. In short, ecological civilization construction will lead to an overall change of the profession of landscape architecture in China.

林学与法学、制度经济学等学科的交叉研究。主要内容为：风景园林法制的一般理论，如制度与风景园林理论实践之关系、风景权理论等；具体法律制度对风景园林的作用，如《土壤污染防治法》对绿地系统的影响；风景园林实践相关的制度建构，如执业注册制度、国家公园与自然保护地立法等。

在实践层面，力推将景观作为一个显性领域纳入生态文明建设，提升到国家战略高度。主要内容为：将景观质量目标/景观特征作为从国土空间规划到场地设计，从环境影响评价到设计导则的所有规划设计领域的实质性考量因素，并将景观特征评估作为空间规划的重要工具。

综上所述，我们必须认识到生态文明建设对于风景园林既是机遇也是挑战。风景园林与其他学科的竞争日趋激烈，竞争学科的范围也将不断扩大。除了规划设计理论，景观设计的核心理论还需要包括管理学、社会学、法学、经济学等学科。简单来说，生态文明将导致中国风景园林行业的整体变革。

# Seeking Evidence-Based Ecological Practice
# 循证生态规划设计

**王志芳 | WANG Zhifang**

Associate Professor, College of Architecture and Landscape Architecture, Peking University. Formerly an assistant professor at Texas A&M University, Wang holds a PhD in Landscape Architecture from University of Michigan and has published over 50 peer-reviewed articles and one book. Her key research interest is in sustainable landscape strategies, including performance assessments with particular regard to ecological science-practice interfaces.

美国密歇根大学自然资源与环境学博士，北京大学建筑与景观设计学院副教授，曾任职于美国德克萨斯A&M大学建筑学院城市与景观规划设计系。她曾在国内外核心期刊上发表论文五十次，并参与完成多项国内外科研类与实践类项目。她的主要研究方向为可持续发展策略及其效益评价，特别是生态科研与实践的错位及解决途径。具体方向包括：可实践生态知识，乡土景观，生态规划设计，绿色基础设施规划设计，生态修复，景观绩效评价等。

Ecological protection and restoration have become key national strategies of China as the nation approaches the era of ecological civilization.[1] The field of landscape architecture has been presented with the opportunity to actively participate in the nation's ascent to ecological civilization through ecological planning and design, even though the use of "ecology" and "sustainability" as slogans and assumptions must be overcome.[2] The impressive ecological research and accomplishments of China over the past few decades have yet to effectively influence the nation's planning and design practices,[3] and poor communication between ecological science and landscape practices has hindered the accessibility and relevance of ecological science to landscape-based decision making. Accordingly, this paper discusses strategies that can be used to successfully implement evidence-based ecological planning and design in China by integrating science and practice and by drawing on the lessons learned through previous ecological studies.

## Epistemology of Evidence-Based Ecological Practice

The great number of ill-designed landscapes across the country that display "planning/designing without ecology"[3] are mainly the result of the gap between ecological research and practice (GERP), which is a global problem that has attracted more and more attention during the last decade. Indeed, *Science* has

published a series of articles that discuss the topic in regard to environmental problems and possible countermeasures,[4] and *Nature-Sustainability* recently established a special committee on the "science-policy interface." Relevant experts in Western countries have summarized the different manifestations of the GERP, have initiated some attempts for solutions (from both theoretical and practical perspectives),[5] and have even tried to integrate landscape planning and design practices into ecological research.[6]

Unlike the heated international discussions, limited attention has been paid to the GERP in China, which deserves attention and collaboration from both researchers and practitioners across multiple disciplines. In light of China's different urban governance mechanism (a top-down and command-control governance regime)[7] and the urgent needs to advance ecological civilization, it may be wise for the landscape industry to first confront the two major components of the GERP,[8] as follows.

(1) *Layman graphics in practice versus technical articles in research.* Landscape planning and design practices rely

中国正进入以生态文明为基础的美丽中国建设新时期，生态规划与修复成为时代发展的重要议题[1]。景观规划设计虽面临重大机遇但却一直无法成为生态文明建设的主力，原因之一就是"生态"与"可持续发展"在规划设计业界常常只是口号与假设，并没有落实到实处[2]。中国过去几十年蓬勃发展的生态科研及相关成果[3]并未能有效指导中国的规划设计实践。如何使中国的生态规划设计变得有理有据、如何使实践过程有机结合借鉴已有的科研成果是我关注的核心议题。

### 认识论：规划设计实践与生态科研的错位

生态科研与实践的错位作为世界性的难题近十年来受到越来越多的重视，《科学》杂志接连发表了一系列文章谈论生态环境问题中实践与科研的错位及可能的应对建议[4]。《自然-可持续发展》杂志最近也成立了一个"生态科研—政策应用(science-policy interface)"方面的专委会。欧美的相关专家从理论和实际操作层面对错位的不同表现以及如何解决两者之间的错位给出一些提议和尝试[5]，甚至试图将规划设计实践融入生态科研中[6]。

与国际上的激烈讨论不同，中国对这个错位尚鲜少有人重视。整体错位的解决之道有赖于不同专业之间的全方位改变与合作，但考虑到中国城市管理机制的不同[7]以及当下生态文明建设的迫切需求，我认为中国景观行业首先要直面“生态科研与规划设计实践”之间的两大核心错位[8]，理清与其他相关专业的关系才能有效参与生态文明建设。这两大错位主要是：

（1）“白话图示与专业文章”的差异，主要是指的是景观规划设计实践需用浅显易懂的图纸、PPT甚至是视频来传达思路以及问题的解决之道。但科研只在专业期刊上发表，且研究问题可能并不针对实践需求，也可能根本没有具体的实践指导建议[9]。(2)“整体系统与解构功能” 的错位，其根本在于现代科学对于还原主义的强化，认为复杂事物可以被分为小的组分来加以理解和描述。例如生态学的下属学科按照生物系统结构分类就有个体生态学、种群生态学、群落生态学等。而景观生态实践划分单元是物质空间，是“场地导向的整体”决策，比如滨水设计、旧城改造、湿地公园等，都要综合考虑多种问题以及功能[10]。以上述两大错位为基础，目前我自己所倡导的“循证生态规划设计“过程也主要有两大对应方法。

### 方法之一：“集成” “白话”科研成果

中国的景观行业不需要去学习做生态科研，却迫切需要以景观为媒[11]，强化对生态科研成果的集成与理解。生态科研已有许多成果散落在各大期刊和报告中。“白话科研”要解决现今科研成果晦涩、解构、缺乏场地针对性的问题，这是散点知识的整合过程，该过程需要实现从“四散结论”到“归集发现”，从“生涩发现”到“直白的问题解决途径”，从“字面解决途径”到“空间图面策略”的转化过程[12]。是将各种零散的专业知识与科研发现转化成设计导则或者空间模式的过程。这一过程最好能够和教学有机结合，在传播知识的过程中归纳集成生态科研成果。

### 方法之二：景观社会服务研究

阻碍中国生态科研有效应用的原因之一就是现有科研过度强化自然过程，而忽视“自然-社会“系统的整体性。我认为对于景观社会服务研究的强化有助于推进生态科研的实践应用。

on straightforward and easy-to-understand drawings, PowerPoint presentations, or even videos to convey ideas and solutions. However, the majority of research findings are only published in specialized journals and present tremendous statistics and charts but limited practical guidance, possibly because many research questions are not specific to practical needs.[9] (2) *Holistic decision in practice versus reductive research in ecology.* This gap lies in the great reductionism in modern science, which holds that complex things can be understood and described as the sum of much smaller components. For example, the subordinate disciplines of ecology can be classified into individual ecology, population ecology, and community ecology according to the structure of the biological system being studied. In contrast, the landscape practice normally works far beyond any one specific ecological perspective and involves site-oriented holistic decisions for broader projects, such as waterfront design, city-center reconstruction, or the construction of wetland parks, all of which must address a variety of issues and functions for integrated decision making.[10] Considering these two gaps, we propose two methods for evidence-based ecological practice.

### Method One: Transitional Research to Synthesize Ecological Findings

There is no urgent need for landscape practitioners in China to learn how to conduct ecological research by themselves. Instead, these practitioners should learn to view landscapes as a medium to which available ecological research results can be applied.[11] However, because many ecological research results have been scattered throughout a variety of journals and reports, transitional research is needed to confront the series of practical barriers that are embedded in ecological science, particularly the reductive research procedure and obscure research findings. Such transitional research should develop a process to synthesize and illustrate ecological science, thereby converting it from scattered conclusions to aggregated discovery, from obscure discovery to straightforward problem-solving approaches, and from literal solutions to illustrated practice strategies. It is the process of transforming the great variety of scattered technical knowledge and scientific research findings into design guidelines or spatial patterns,[12] to transcend purely scientific concerns and to provide practitioners with solid and science-based decision guidelines. This process can best be achieved through teaching during knowledge dissemination.

**Method Two: Research of Landscape Social Services**

One of the issues that hinders the effective application of ecological research in China is that existing scientific research over-emphasizes natural processes and tends to ignore the integrity of the "natural-social" system. Therefore, strengthening landscape social service research will help promote the practical application of ecological research.

Landscape social services are defined on the basis of ecosystem cultural services:[13] the intangible benefits that society receives from the ecosystem through spiritual enrichment, cognitive development, reflection, entertainment, and aesthetic experience. By using the term landscape social services, the research emphasis of my team is laid on landscape and social values because cultural services in China will directly provoke the protection of history and culture. Landscape social services refer more to the recreational and aesthetic functions that natural resources can provide for society than to the protection of cultural relics.

The significance of landscape social service research lies in the fact that social service is the core requirement of human habitat, yet, it is not well addressed by ecological scientists, particularly in China. Meanwhile, landscape architects are not necessarily involved in the protection and restoration of natural places, where there is no requirement for social values, owing to limited human use. For the restoration of pure natural environments, there are countless ecologists who know better about nature, and nature can also restore itself after disturbance.[14] The goal of landscape architecture is to balance ecological restoration and social services in human settlements.

Three research methods can be used to explore landscape social services. First, expert-driven methods, which are

景观社会服务是以生态系统文化服务[13]为基础进行界定的:人们从生态系统中通过精神充实、认知发展、反思、娱乐和审美体验获得的非物质利益。强调"景观"与"社会"是因为在中国"文化服务"直接会走入历史文化保护,这里更多指自然资源能为社会提供的游憩与审美等功能,不是文物保护。

景观社会服务研究的意义在于它是人居环境改善的核心,却不为生态科研所重视。同时对于景观实践而言,在没有社会文化价值建构的地方进行保护与修复,不需要景观设计师。纯生态的事情,自然可以自己做功还有无数的生态学家[14]。建构景观社会文化服务体系是景观行业了解自己对人居环境构建价值的途径之一。

研究方法主要有三种:(1)以指标为基础的专家打分法,大尺度的项目更实用,操作简单明了,能够快速构建整体"面"上的体系。(2)以现场实测与问卷为基础的使用者调研法,更试用于场地尺度,费时费力,属于"点"上的详细信息。(3)以多维网络资源为基础的大数据分析法,技术要求较高,却有将使用者意见由点变为面的潜力。这些不同的方法可以应用到不同的项目。

应用一,扬长避短的空间规划。当今中国地方政府的一大诉求就是把"绿水青山"转变为"金山银山"。这一过程的核心是生态产品,其界定有赖于对于自然资源生态价值以及社会文化价值的综合理解。目前我们已经结合生态安全格局和社会文化价值评价体系,尝试如何在县域建构绿色基础设施体系、构建景观管理单元体系并明确重点生态产品、生态修复及空间整理重点区域。

应用二,发现问题并提出解决途径与修复策略。景观社会文化服务的质量直接反应了使用者对于人居环境的满意程度。结合网络大数据分析和现场调研,可以直接了解问题所在区域(社会文化服务极低或负面),并能够部分提炼影响要素,进而对城市更新以及生态修复提出直接的策略与建设意见。我们已在北京和广州市进行了相关应用[15]。

**结语**

以生态文明为基础的美丽中国建设有赖于全方位的跨学科合作。景观行业需要强化对已有生态研究成果的归纳总结,并通过自己的研究去弥补现有体系中的缺口,进而推进有理有据的生态规划与生态修复实践。

based on selected indicators, are generally more appropriate for large-scale projects as they focus on creating a general framework for a place. Second, user-based methods, which rely on field measurements and questionnaires that are relatively time- and labor-consuming, are more applicable for the "point analysis" of small sites, as they provide detailed information and in-depth exploration. And third, multi-sourced big data, which is a recently emerged strategy, provides new opportunities to transmit users' opinions from small "points" to large-area "surfaces," thereby better aligning user opinions with large-scale analysis and decision-making. Of course, these different approaches can be applied to different projects.

One of the applications of such methods is spatial planning. The call for transforming "green mountains" to "golden and silver mountains" by President Xi has become the core of local decision-making across China. To operationalize this policy, local decision-making will rely on a comprehensive understanding of local landscapes' ecological and social values. A framework and methodology for examining landscape social services provide fundamental knowledge and appreciation of local environments. Indeed, we have used such methods to develop regional green infrastructure and landscape management systems in several projects.

The other application is to identify the key issues deserving immediate attention during urban renewal. In a development period when China's urbanization rate has reached 60%, many Chinese cities are in need of renewal and renovation, in order to meet the population's growing demand for a better quality of life. Landscape social services directly reflect the satisfaction of users within their living environments. Therefore, by combining big data analysis and field investigations, in-depth analyses of landscape social services can identify problematic regions (landscape social services are very low or negative), shed light onto relevant influential factors, and then propose specific strategies and construction suggestions for urban renewal and ecological restoration. Pilot studies have been performed by my team on the basis of multi-sourced data from Beijing and Guangzhou.[15]

## Conclusion

Building a beautiful China on the basis of ecological civilization would rely on multifaceted cross-disciplinary collaborations. To launch and prepare for the collaboration process for landscape architecture, the landscape industry needs to strengthen the synthesis of available ecological results, and then utilize individual research to better align practice desires with the gaps in the existing research. Ultimately, it is the coupling of practical knowledge and ecological research that can promote ecologically sound planning and ecological restoration practices, and thus contribute to the national strategy of ecological civilization.

1. Wang Z., "Evolving Landscape-Urbanization Relationships in Contemporary China," *Landscape and Urban Planning* 171 (2018): 30–41.
2. Wu J., "Urban Ecology and Sustainability," *Landscape and Urban Planning*, 125 (2014): 209–21.
3. Wu J., Xiang W.N. & Zhao J., "Urban Ecology in China: Historical developments and future directions," *Landscape and Urban Planning*, 125 (2014): 222–33.
4. Briggs S.V. & Knight A.T., "Science-Policy Interface: Scientific Input Limited," Science 333, no. 6043 (2011): 696–97; Grimm N.B., et al., "Global Change and the Ecology of Cities," *Science* 319, no. 5864 (2008): 756–60; Nisbet M.C. & Mooney C., "Framing Science," *Science* 316, no. 5821 (2007): 56.
5. Beunen R. & Opdam P., "When Landscape Planning Becomes Landscape Governance, What Happens to the Science?" *Landscape and Urban Planning* 100 (2011): 324–26; Braunisch C., et al., "Conservation Science Relevant to Action: A research agenda identified and prioritized by practitioners," *Biological Conservation* 153 (2012): 201–10; Opdam P., et al., "Science for Action at the Local Landscape Scale," *Landscape Ecology* 28 (2013): 1439–45.
6. Nassauer J.I. & Opdam P., "Design in Science: Extending the landscape ecology paradigm," *Landscape Ecology* 23 (2008): 633–44.
7. Wang Z., et al., "Perspectives on Bridging the Action Gap between Landscape Science and Metropolitan Governance: Practice in the US and China," *Landscape and Urban Planning* 125 (2014): 329–34.
8. Wang Z., "Bridging the Gaps Between Landscape Design Practice and Scientific Research: A graphical intervention," *Landscape Architecture Frontiers* 6, no. 5 (2019): 66–71.
9. Wang Z. & Li M., "How to Frame Design Research Paradigm of Landscape Architecture?" *Chinese Landscape Architecture* 4 (2016): 10–15.
10. Wang Z., "Ecophronesis and Actionable Ecological Knowledge," *Urban Planning International* 4 (2017):12–16; Wang Z. & Shen N., "The Ecological Value of Local Knowledge," *Acta Ecologica Sinica* 38, no. 2 (2018): 371–79.
11. Nassauer, J.I., "Landscape as Medium and Method for Synthesis in Urban Ecological Design," *Landscape and Urban Planning* 106 (2012): 221–29.
12. Wang & Li, "How to Frame Design Research…," ibid; Wang, "Bridging the Gaps…," ibid.
13. Millennium Ecosystem Assessment, Ecosystems and Human Well-Being: Synthesis (Island Press: Washington DC, 2005); Fish R., Church A. & Winter M., "Conceptualizing Cultural Ecosystem Services: A novel framework for research and critical engagement," *Ecosystem Services* 21 (2016): 208–17.
14. Wang Z. & Hou J., "Role of Landscape Design in Place Making for Sustainability," *China Population, Resources and Environment* 24 (2014): 365–68.
15. Wang Z., et al., "Comparing Social Media Data and Survey Data in Assessing the Attractiveness of Beijing Olympic Forest Park" (2018); Wang Z., et al., "Using Ecosystem Disservice as a Framework to Diagnose Urban Problems," *Landscape Architecture Frontiers* 6, no. 30 (2017): 8–16.

# Constructing an Ecological Civilization
# 建设一种生态文明

**理查德.韦勒** | Richard WELLER

Professor and Chair of Landscape Architecture, Meyerson Chair of Urbanism, and co-executive director of the McHarg Center at The University of Pennsylvania. Weller has published over 100 academic papers and six books and his creative work has received numerous awards in international design competitions. In 2017 and 2018, Weller was named by DesignIntelligence as one of North America's most admired teachers of design. His research has focused on scenario planning for cities, megaregions, and nations, and most recently, on global flashpoints between biodiversity and urban growth.

宾夕法尼亚大学景观系主任与伊恩.迈克哈格中心联合执行总裁。韦勒教授发表了超过100篇学术论文与6本著作，他富有创造性的工作已经在国际上收获了无数的荣誉。在2017与2018年度，都被美国权威设计网站“设计智慧”提名为“北美最受尊敬的教师”。他重点研究城市，大区域，以及国家尺度上的规划，最近开始也在重点研究全球范围内的物种多样性与都市增长的热点。

As cities grow larger and larger, their connections with other urban areas lead to networked regions that share economies and ecologies, and often a central vision. These regions have become known as "megaregions." In China, there are three megaregions – the Yangtze River Delta, the Pearl River Delta, and Jing-Jin-Ji. Encompassing Beijing, Tianjin, and Hebei Province in northeastern China, the Jing-Jin-Ji megaregion was the subject of a recent interdisciplinary study and studio at the University of Pennsylvania Weitzman School of Design. This essay describes the landscape findings of that endeavor.

Successful megaregions have several key characteristics: they are economic powerhouses offering a wide range of employment opportunities; they are well connected in terms of transportation and communication systems; they present a range of housing and lifestyle options from dense inner-city zones to open peri-urban and rural landscapes; and they are political and cultural hubs serving, ideally, as incubators of innovation. But none of these are possible unless the megaregion is embedded in a healthy natural environment. While scholarship and policy related to megaregions typically focus on urban areas, it is the surrounding landscape that ultimately underpins and sustains a megaregion, offering benefits to citizens in the form of clean air, water, and food. Therefore, as China's central government moves to construct and link the urban fabric of the Jing-Jin-Ji megaregion, it must also undertake the restoration of the region's depleted landscapes.

The Jing-Jin-Ji landscape faces an interconnected set of problems concerning air and water quality, multiple forms of pollution, loss of habitat, loss of productive soil, and depletion of the groundwater supplies. Air pollution is perhaps the most visible and well-known environmental problem facing Jing-Jin-Ji. On the calendar day marked as the most severe in the last few years, the concentration of PM2.5 rose to 50 times the accepted healthy limit. Cities at the southern end of the Hebei Province are particularly affected by air pollution and, as a result, ailments connected to air quality are widespread and life expectancies are lower here than the national average. The most significant factors contributing to such levels of pollution are coal-fired power stations, outdated industrial practices, coal-based domestic heating, and growing vehicle ownership.

Water scarcity and pollution are also critical concerns in the Jing-Jin-Ji megaregion. The major rivers and riparian zones that traverse the megaregion from east to west are polluted and ecologically dysfunctional. The megaregion has limited surface water, much of which is polluted by the expansion of impervious surfaces and a lack of storm-water-related controls. The lack of surface water and the poor quality of this water has recently been addressed by the South–North Water Transfer project, which brings water from the water-rich south to the arid north. However, taking from the south to give to the north is not a viable long-term solution to national water scarcity. In Jing-Jin-Ji, the aquifer is being depleted across the region, so much so that in places the land and related infrastructure is subsiding. Much of the groundwater and surface water quality is poor due to pollution from agricultural and industrial sources. The Bohai Bay—the region's main coastal resource and receiving environment for the region's catchment—presents twin issues: critical levels of pollution and the looming reality of sea level rise. Sea level rise will significantly complicate Tianjin's port-related logistics and throws current regional plans, which emphasize further rapid development along the coastal belt, into question.

The megaregion's population growth is paired with sprawled and disorderly urban and suburban development that consumes arable land, destroys remnant habitat, and

随着城市的不断扩张，城市之间的连接将形成由中心城市开始辐射的共享经济与生态的城市网络。这些区域往往被称为“大城市群”。在中国有三个大城市群，分别是长三角区域，珠三角区域与京津冀区域。覆盖了中国东北部的北京，天津与河北省的京津冀大城市群是宾夕法尼亚大学威兹曼设计学院一个跨学科核心设计课的研究主题。本文将描述在这一主题下京津冀大城市群的景观学发现。

一个成功的大城市群往往有几个重要特征：拥有能提供大量不同工作岗位的经济体；拥有完善的交通与通讯网络；能提供由密集中心城区，低密度郊区到农业景观的一系列不同的居住与生活方式的选择；在城市群中存在区域政治或文化中心，理想化来说，存在创新孵化中心。但如果缺乏一个健康的自然环境基础，这些特性都不可能会存在。当学术研究与发展决策往往关注与城市化区域时，其实是城市周边的景观空间在不断支持与巩固中心区域的发展，为城市居民提供新鲜的空气，水和食物。因此，当中国的中央政府投入建设与连接京津冀大城市区时，它必须同时投入于区域中日渐恶化的景观环境的修复之中。

京津冀的景观环境面临着一系列相互关联的生态问题，包括空气与水的质量问题，多种污染问题，栖息地的丧失，土壤肥力的丧失和地下水供给的减少。其中空气污染也许是最为可见与广为人知的一个环境问题。在过去几年空气污染最严重的日子里，空气中PM2.5的含量已经达到了不影响人体健康PM2.5浓度极限的50倍。河北省南部的城市受空气污染的影响最为严重，与空气污染相关的疾病在这些城市中十分常见，并且这些城市的人均寿命也低于国家平均水平。造成如此严重的空气污染的成因包括了大量的火力发电站，落后的工业生产方式，以煤炭燃烧为暖气来源的供暖系统和不断增长的私家车使用。

水资源的匮乏与污染问题也是京津冀区域的一个主要生态问题。由东至西穿越过整个大城市区域的主要河流与河流沿岸区域都受到了一定程度的污染，其生态功能也受到了损害。京津冀生态区有着非常有限的地表水资源，并且大部分地表水由于区域中不断增加的不可渗透表面的增加与雨洪管理设施的缺乏受到了污染。近年来，地表水的缺乏与污染问题被南水北调

*The JERA Process*
京津冀生态保护管理委员会

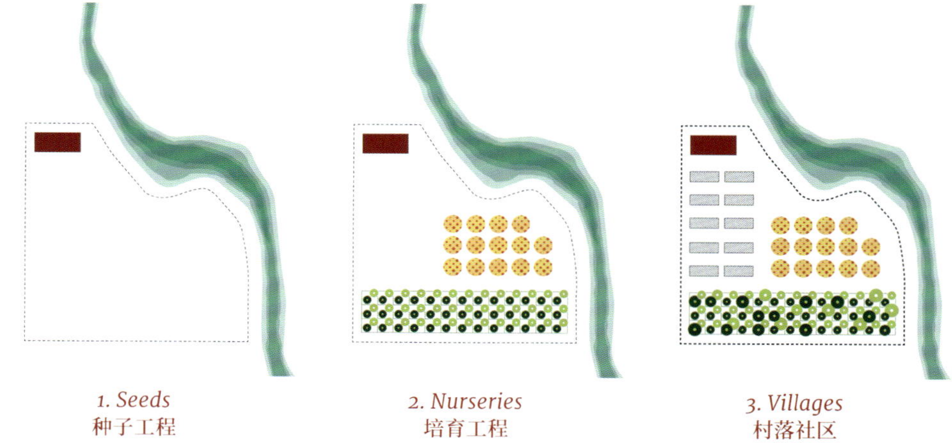


工程所缓解，即从中国南部水资源充沛的区域输送水资源到干涸的北部。

大城市群的人口增长往往伴随着城市与城市郊区的蔓延与无秩序发展，这些发展往往会侵蚀可耕种的土地，剩余的生物栖息地和形成排水系统的硬化与渠化。可耕种土地与森林的减少给京津冀区域带来了以下几个负面影响，其中包括土壤的盐化，酸化，水土流失与沙尘暴，这些负面影响会进一步的影响土壤质量与农业产出。贫困农业地区传统的农业耕作方式与经济压力也同样造成了土壤质量进一步恶化与水体的富营养化。除此之外，在经过了30年的持续的快速城市化之后，该区域的生物多样性已经显著减少。除了山区以外，京津冀地区也明显缺乏具有一定规模的可自给自足的生态保护区域和景观连接通道。

因此，为了保护与修复具有生物多样性的栖息地，从而为京津冀地区提供更高质量的空气和水与旅游休闲活动资源，我们能做些什么呢？ 通过研究，我们假设建立了一个新的政府部门——京津冀生态保护管理委员会(JERA)，该组织通过将一套新的生态系统整合到

mechanizes drainage patterns. The loss of arable and forestland has brought several negative repercussions to the region, including soil salination, erosion, aridity, and sandstorms that further affect the quality of the soils and the agricultural yields. Low-tech agricultural practices and economic stress on the rural poor also result in land degradation and eutrophication of waterways. Additionally, after almost 30 years of sustained rapid urbanization, the region's biodiversity has suffered significant losses and is now virtually devoid of viable protected areas and forms of landscape connectivity on a meaningful scale, except for mountainous hinterlands.

So, what can be done to protect and restore biodiverse habitats to provide for improved air and water quality and recreation opportunities for residents of the Jing-Jin-Ji megaregion? Our study proposed the establishment of a new government department—the Jing-Jin-Ji Eco-Region Authority (JERA)—with the mandate to reconstruct ecological functionality on a megaregional scale and integrate this new ecology with urban development and

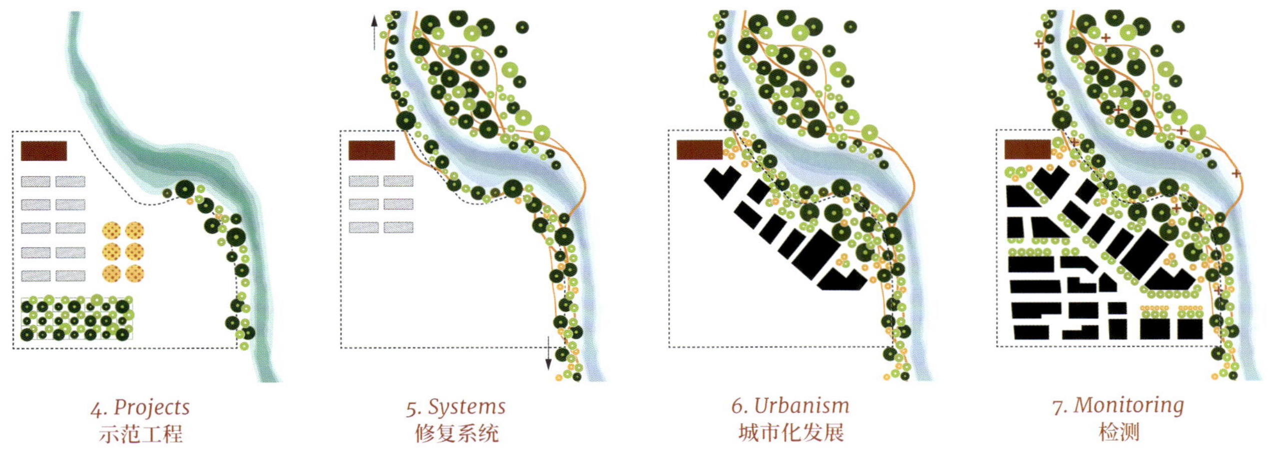

4. Projects
示范工程

5. Systems
修复系统

6. Urbanism
城市化发展

7. Monitoring
检测

infrastructure. It was proposed that JERA would be guided by three overarching aims: first, to articulate and manifest the ideals of ecological civilization as a transformative cultural and ecological project of historical significance to China and the world; second, to reconstruct a functional ecosystem at the Jing-Jin-Ji megaregional scale – one that delivers the fundamental ecological services of clean air, clean water, and clean food and one which significantly enhances the biodiversity of the region and provides natural amenity, beauty, and security for all the citizens and species of the Jing-Jin-Ji; and third, to integrate the reconstruction of the Jing-Jin-Ji megaregion's ecosystem with urban development and its associated infrastructures. JERA's method for reconstructing the Jing-Jin-Ji megaregion's ecosystem would be achieved through the seven steps described below.

**Step 1: Seeds**

The "seeds" are small ecological research and design laboratories established in strategic sites throughout the

城市的发展与基础建设之中，来重建京津冀地区的生态功能。JERA的工作将被统领于三个相互交叉的目标之下：第一，声明与强调生态文明是一个关系到中国和世界文化转变的重要生态工程；第二，为京津冀区域的居民和生物，重建一套既能够提供新鲜的空气，水，安全的食物，又能够有效的增加区域的生态多样性和提供自然风景，休闲活动和安全的基础生态服务设施；第三，整合京津冀区域的生态系统重建工作到城市的发展和基础设施的建设中。JERA重建京津冀地区的生态系统的目标将有以下描述的七个步骤来实现。

**第一步：种子工程**

种子工程是在京津冀地区范围内的七个景观类型区域中选择出来的战略性场地所设置小型生态研究与设计实验室。这些种子工程的选址的确定是因为他们能够代表京津冀地区的生态多样性情况。每个种子工程分别提供驻地的生态学家，工程师，规划师与景观师团队分别从事数据收集和JERA生态修复工作的实验项目的工作。每个种子工程作为生态修复工作的总部进行研究，设计，并在“种子”的“种植”阶段，最终从事生态修复工作的实际操作。这些种子工程同时也将作为文化中心来保持JERA与周边社区信息的交换，使JERA能够不断从实践中汲取经验并不断对自身的工作进行检测与自我修正。这些种子工程会与全球范围内参与京津冀生态系统修复工作的高校与咨询顾问保持密切的交流，形成全球第一个与最大的生态区域重建活动。

**第二步：培育工程**

在种子工程周边的开放空间，培育工程将培养所有的植物和储存所需的材料，来满足在周边进行的JERA生态修复工作的需要。通过这种方式，植物的储存量将在场地内达到保证，并且这些植物将适应于当地的微气候。这些培育工程也将为当地希望同步参与到JERA生态修复工作中的社区提供植物材料和项目建议。

**第三：村落社区**

村落社区是与种子工程与培育工程相连接的，所有JERA的职工可以接受培训的区域，如果职工不来自于当地的社区，职工们也可以居住在村落社区中。这些村落社区的结构与设计与中国许多的大型基建项目的工人社区相似。

**第四步：示范工程**

示范工程是建立于第一级种子——培育——村落社区系统周边的工程范本，并且将在尺度上不断增加成为实际的生态修复工程。由于京津冀地区大部分自然景观都已被开发或在某种程度经过了人为的改造，所以这些示范工程将成为理解何种生态修复技术能够在区域的特定环境下成功的最好的试验场所。当一个项目完成时，种子——培育——村落社区系统将移动到下一个修复场地，循环以往，直到所有示范工程能够共同形成一个连贯的景观系统。

**第五步：修复系统**

京津冀修复系统将整合所有单独的修复项目形成一个在更大尺度上的具有弹性的景观网络。 当一个单

seven landscape types of the entire Jing-Jin-Ji megaregion. The locations for the seeds are chosen because together they represent the diversity of ecological conditions found in the Jing-Jin-Ji megaregion. Each seed provides the onsite infrastructure for teams of ecologists, engineers, planners, and landscape architects to work together on gathering the data and creating the pilot projects for JERA's ecological restoration work. Each seed functions as the headquarters for the research, the design, and ultimately the works required to reconstruct the ecosystem in which the seed is "planted." The seeds would also function as cultural centers relaying information between JERA and surrounding communities, enabling JERA to "learn by doing" and to constantly monitor and self-correct its methods. The seeds would be connected to a global network of universities and consultants all involved in the Jing-Jin-Ji restoration project – the world's first and largest single attempt to reconstruct an entire ecoregion.

**Step 2: Nurseries**

The nurseries, sited in open space adjacent to the seeds, would cultivate all the plants and store other materials required for the JERA ecological restoration project that will take place in the surrounding land. In this way, plant stock is hardened in situ and can adapt to local microclimatic conditions. The nurseries would also provide plant material and advice to local community groups wishing to undertake their own projects of ecological restoration in sync with JERA's work.

**Step 3: Villages**

The villages are connected to the seeds and the nurseries and are where JERA employees are educated in landscape restoration techniques and where they can live if they are not from the local community. The villages are designed and constructed similarly to worker camps, typical to major construction projects in China.

**Step 4: Projects**

The projects are demonstration sites established nearby the primary seed-nursery-village complex, which begin

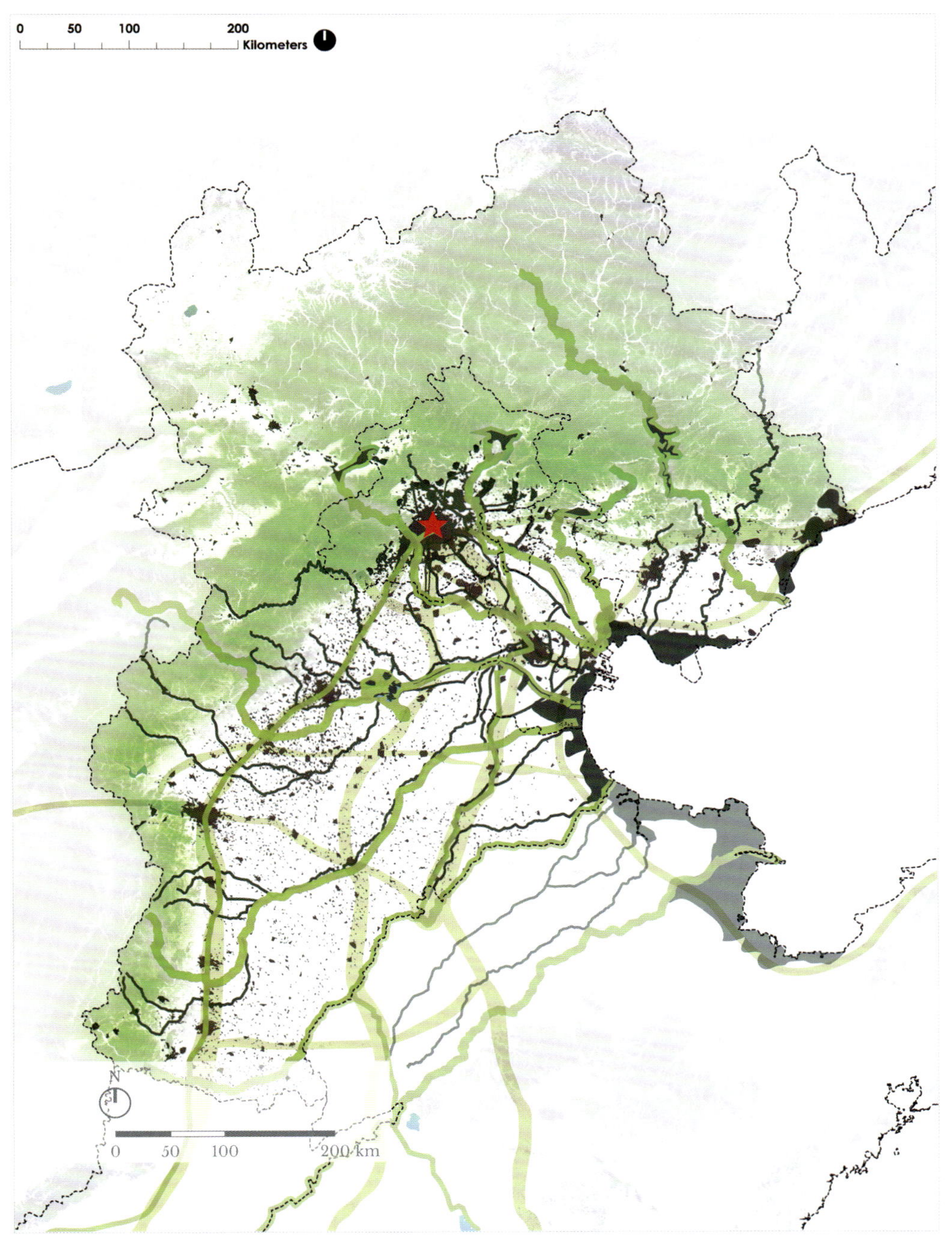


JERA 通过生态修复创造相互联系的景观网络格局

The JERA process aims to create an interconnected landscape matrix.

独的生态修复项目的上游或周边区域有着不匹配的土地利用方式时，JERA发起的修复工作将无法达到最好的效果。所以，应将每一个修复项目置于更大的生态网络中考量和更大的生态系统中评价其修复效益。

### 第六步：城市化发展

这是一个城市化发展的阶段，指的是由JERA建议的区域中能够在生态价值，社会价值与经济价值上与修复后的景观互相促进的城市化发展机会和提出的城市设计导则。这些城市化发展将利用周边修复后景观所形成的具有良好生态服务功能的健康生态系统和公众休闲空间的价值来指导城市开发利用。

### 第七步：检测

为了更好的理解区域内的景观绩效，JERA生态修复工程所发起的种子工程也将作为京津冀地区未来长期的景观生态监控中心。通过持续的观察，JERA将建立完善的询证生态修复知识系统，同时也能够帮助中国与世界其它地区希望进行类似生态重建工作的区域。

### 结论

近年来，中国的城市化进程在很大程度上排除了对生态问题的考虑。但是，随着中国景观专业的发展，这种情况正在改变。人们的环境意识正在不断增强，景观生态学和人类健康与城市形态的设计和建造之间的联系日益受到重视。生态文明和美丽中国的概念重申了这种环境意识，同时，相关政策也使这些概念不仅仅停留于理论阶段。随着21世纪的到来，中国有能力开展国家尺度上的生态修复计划，以恢复其具有悠久历史的景观环境的健康和活力。而本文中提出的方案也是宾夕法尼亚大学威兹曼设计学院的学生和教师，以京津冀大城市群为例，对此类大型生态修复项目应如何启动与管理的一种畅想与建议。

to phase-in the actual restorative work at scale. Because almost the entire landscape of the Jing-Jin-Ji is already heavily developed or modified in one way or another, these demonstration projects are important testbeds for understanding which restorative techniques will succeed in particular situations. As the projects take shape, JERA stays one step ahead coordinating land resumption and removing incompatible land uses by way of preparing future sites for the restorative work. When a project is completed, the seeds, nurseries, and villages move to their next location, and so on, until the projects can be strung together into coherent landscape systems.

### Step 5: Systems

The systems are formed by joining together smaller individual projects into larger more resilient landscape networks. It makes little sense to restore a site here when either upstream or adjacent to it are incompatible land uses that will negate the restorative work that JERA has started. In this sense, each individual project has to be tied into a larger network or system of restorative measures.

### Step 6: Urbanism

This is the development phase, where JERA identifies development opportunities aand oversees urban designs, which are coupled with the restored landscapes in a way that is ecologically, socially, and economically compatible. These developments will derive value from the restored landscape and public amenity of a functional, healthy ecosystem in the immediate vicinity.

### Step 7: Monitoring

The seeds with which JERA's ecological restoration project began also function as monitoring centers for better understanding landscape performance over the long term. Through the process of constant monitoring the ERA is able to develop evidence-based knowledge that can be disseminated to help guide similar reconstruction efforts in other parts of China and the rest of the world.

## Conclusion

The pace of China's recent urbanization has largely precluded development practices that incorporate ecological concerns. However, along with the maturation of the landscape architecture profession in China, this is now changing. Environmental awareness is growing and the connections between landscape ecology and human health in relation to the design and construction of urban form are increasingly appreciated. The concepts and related policies of ecological civilization and Beautiful China manifest this awareness and make it not only possible, but probable that China will be able to undertake a coordinated national project of restoring the health and vitality of its ancient landscape as the 21st century unfolds. This proposal by the students and faculty of the University of Pennsylvania Weitzman School of Design offers a sketch of how such a process might be initiated and managed in the case of the Jing-Jin-Ji megaregion.

Acknowledgments: Special thanks to team members Lucia Artavia, Siyang Jing, Alma Siulagi, Boqian Xu, Alyssa Garcia, and Zhangkan Zhou. This study was undertaken as a part of an interdisciplinary studio looking at a broad range of issues regarding the Jing-Jin-Ji megaregion at the University of Pennsylvania Weitzman School of Design codirected by Richard Weller, Marilyn Taylor, and Robert Yaro.

鸣谢：特别感谢团队成员卢西亚·阿塔维亚，景斯阳，阿拉马·休拉基，徐搏谦，阿莉萨·哥西亚和周张侃。这项研究是跨学科设计课程的一部分，该课程主要研究京津冀特大城市群中的城市问题，由理查德·韦勒，玛丽莲·泰勒和罗伯特·雅罗联合主持。

生產景觀

# 生产景观
# The Working Landscape

# The Evolution of China's Polder Landscapes
# 中国传统圩田景观研究

**郭巍 | GUO Wei**

Associate Professor, School of Landscape Architecture, Beijing Forestry University. Guo has led a number of research projects funded by the National Natural Science Foundation of China, the National Social Science Foundation of China, the Beijing Natural Science Foundation, the Beijing Social Science Foundation, and the Humanities and Social Sciences Foundation of the Ministry of Education. He has published over 30 articles and his design projects have earned awards of excellence from the Chinese Society of Landscape Architecture and the International Federation of Landscape Architects Asia-Pacific.

北京林业大学园林学院副教授。研究领域主要为中国传统人居环境。主持和参与国家自科基金、国家社科基金、北京自然科学基金、北京社科基金、教育部人文社科基金等近10项；在核心和重要期刊发表学术论文超过30篇，相关文章获得风景园林学会佳作等奖项；主持和参与设计实践项目超过30项，并多次获得IFLA亚太杰出奖等奖项。

A polder is an irrigated field that is shaped and managed to resist floods by building dikes and renovating water systems in low-lying landscapes. Polders are then networked together to form vast and more-complex "polder landscapes" for the purpose of water conservancy, farming, and construction of settlements. China's polder landscapes (such as those in the middle and lower reaches of the Yangtze River) are symbiotic with traditional culture and involve a long history of land reclamation. For example, the mulberry fish pond—a unique type of Chinese polder, which is widely distributed in the Yangtze River Delta and the Pearl River Delta—has existed since the 16th century. This essay describes the evolution of polder reclamation in China and its structural characteristics, and takes Ningshao Plain as a case study to understand and appreciate polder landscapes so as to better manage their future.

Water is the most important shaping force in the polder landscape. Water in all its forms from the coast to inland rivers is carefully directed through precise earthworks. The complex water system consisting of seawalls and dikes, canals and ponds, sluices and dams has transformed vast swampy regions into a stable and fertile high-yield agricultural and urbanized landscape. Water systems of various scales and grades have also become the basis for subdivision of reclaimed polder land for different functions, and different soil conditions have produced diverse types of polders.

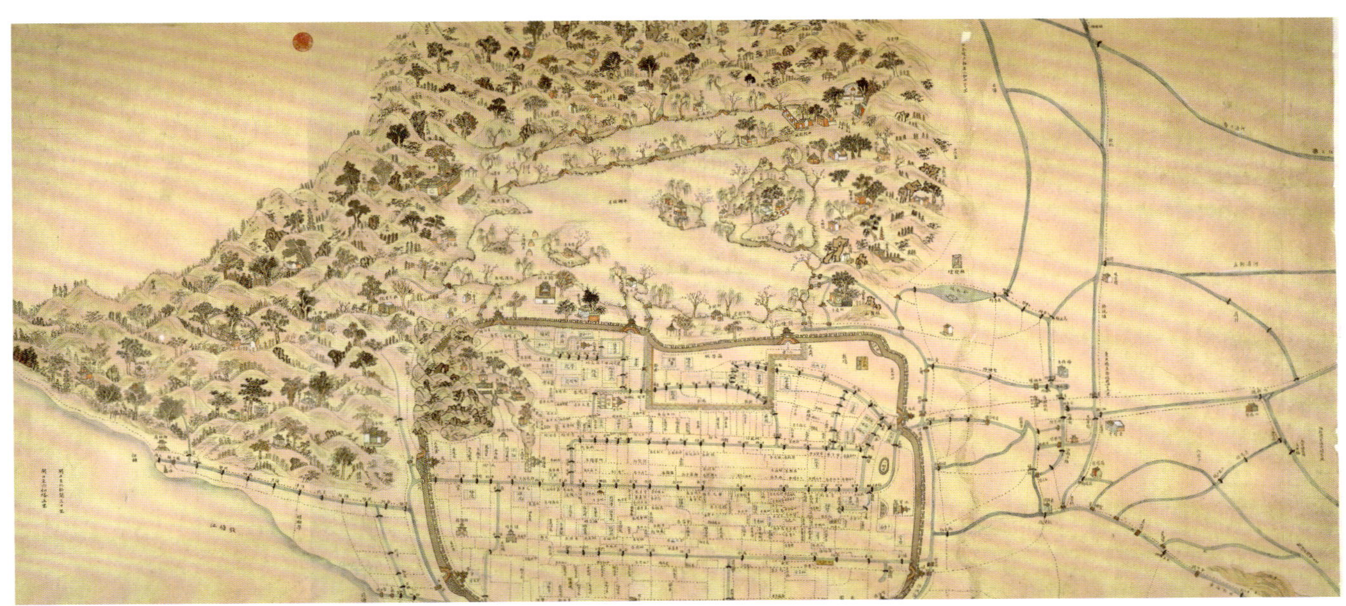

杭州城市形态发展与圩田开垦有关

The form and development of Hangzhou is closely related to polder reclamation

Due to the high yields of polder landscapes, these areas have also historically become the most urbanized. In areas such as the Yangtze River Delta, both the polders and the city have a common environmental foundation and a similar development history. The shape of the polders and the urban form are closely linked. It can be said that each polder is basically an urban project and vice versa.[1] The traditional Chinese scholar class plays an important role in this, and has presided over a number of comprehensive plans including water conservancy, polder reclamation, and urban construction, reflecting the high degree of integration of urban planning, landscape architecture, and hydrology.

The polder constitutes an important part of China's human-made wetlands and its landscape quality and agricultural functions have long been praised. The polder landscape has therefore become an integral part of China's traditional landscape architecture practice. For example, the construction of traditional scenery such as the West Lake is closely related to the polder reclamation in the Hangzhou-Jiaxing-Huzhou Plain, and the influence of polder landscape design can also be found in the planning and design of traditional gardens such as the Yuanmingyuan (Old Summer Palace) in Beijing.

圩田是在低洼的沼泽水网地带，通过筑堤和改造水系，内以围田、外以挡水的水利田，并进而整合形成面积巨大、更为复杂的圩田景观。圩田景观是水利、农耕和聚落营建的综合，具有水文流域、空间地域和社区组织的多重特征，是低洼河网地区传统的人居环境单元，在我国长江中下游以及滨海平原等地分布较为广泛。我国特有的圩田类型—桑基鱼塘则是其中的典型，自16世纪开始广泛存在于长三角和珠三角。文章简述中国圩田开垦的沿革，阐述其分层结构特征，并以宁绍平原为例，分析圩田景观为主体的传统人居环境营建。

水是圩田景观最重要的塑造力量。地形和高差的变化，以及由此而决定的自然排水方式和河流网络以及海岸线的变迁等构成了中国传统圩田景观的基础。由海塘和圩堤、运河和陂塘、水闸和堰坝组成的复杂水利系统则成为圩田景观的支撑体系，将原先流动荒芜的沼泽转化为稳定富饶的圩田景观。各个尺度和等级的水利系统也成为圩田开垦和土地划分的依据，不同的水土条件和开垦模式，产生了多样化的圩田类型。

圩田中的聚落结构受制于圩田开垦和水利调控，城镇是圩田村落的放大。在长三角等圩田开发历史较为悠久的地区，圩田和城市有共同的环境基础和相似的发展历史，圩田形态和城市形态紧密相连，可以说每一块圩田从根本上说都是一个城市项目，反之亦然[1]。作为一种农业景观，其丰产美学很早就为士人阶层所接受。

圩田构成了我国次生湿地的重要部分，其风景品质自古以来就就为人称颂。因此，圩田景观也是我国传统风景园林的一个组成部分。例如西湖等传统风景营建都与杭嘉湖平原的圩田开垦密切相关，甚至影响到了圆明园等传统园林的规划设计。

宁绍平原历史上是我国湖泊密度最高的地区，遍布盐沼湿地，《禹贡》将其土地生产能力评价为下下等。2000年前开始在绍兴南部开始开垦，逐渐向北部滨海推进，并延伸到宁波，到15世纪，已经"湖田日辟，屋庐坟墓日稠，千村万聚，一望如屯云"[2]，成为中国最富裕和城市化程度最高的地区之一。

从海塘—运河系統的演变过程可以解读出圩田开垦的依次推进，其发展也是并圩连圩、逐渐整合扩大的过程。宁绍平原圩田开垦由于不同的土壤结构、水文条件以及开垦组织方式而呈现出多样的面貌，圩子形态和尺度差异比较大，但在部分圩区则有明显设计的特征，带有很强的模数痕迹。宁绍平原城镇体系依据在陂塘-运河网-海塘这一水利系统中的等级、区位等差异以及圩田的土地划分，形成了闸堰聚落、堤塘聚落和圩子聚落等具有微妙结构差异的聚落体系。作为中心城市的宁波和绍兴则体现了传统营城模式和有机的圩田景观的结合，宁波日月湖区域的形态结构和发展更是圩田开垦在城内的延伸。

两千年的圩田开垦几乎将这些原本低洼荒芜的土地经过了"设计"，圩田开垦的逻辑贯穿了这些地区传统人居环境的塑造，使得这些地区的农田水利、土地划分、聚落营建和风景经营高度的整合在一起，创造出富饶、丰产的区域景观。而它们不同的自然景观以及人工干预方式的差异，也形成了具有不同景观和人文特征的圩区。对圩田景观的分析，有助于在目前城市化背景下获得圩田景观保护及转型以及城市发展的有益启示。

The Ningshao Plain has the highest density of lakes in China, spread throughout a landscape of salt marshes. In terms of productivity, the Yu Gong referred to this land as the worst performing in China. Two thousand years ago, it began to reclaim in the south of Shaoxing and gradually advanced to the northern coast and extended to Ningbo. By the 15th century, it had become one of the most productive landscapes replete with thriving villages,[2] making it one of the most affluent and urbanized areas in China.

From the evolution of the seawall-canal system, we can interpret the progression of the polder reclamation. Due to different soil structure, hydrological conditions, and reclamation techniques, the polder reclamation of Ningshao Plain has a diverse appearance. The shape and scale of each polder unit is quite different, but some areas show great regularity in respect of design features. The urban system of Ningshao Plain is based on the gradients and infrastructure of the water system of the pond-canal network and the land divisions of polders, forming a settlement pattern with subtle structural differences such as weir-sluice settlements, dike-pond settlements, and polder settlements. Ningbo and Shaoxing, as the central cities, embody the combination of traditional urban construction patterns and organic polder landscapes. The morphological structure and development of the Ningbo Sun Moon Lake area is an extension of polder reclamation in the city.

For two thousand years, the process of constructing the polder system in China has effectively "designed" these low-lying and barren lands. The logic of the polder reclamation process in these areas has influenced the integration of farmland, water conservancy, land subdivision, settlement construction, and landscape management creating a rich and productive regional landscape. The differences in their natural landscapes and the technological limitations of manual labor have resulted in mosaics of different polder typologies with cultural characteristics. It is my contention that deeper analysis of the polder landscape will not only help with protecting and managing these landscapes into the future, but also provide insights into how we may better relate nature, technology, labor, and urbanization in the broader, contemporary landscape.

1. Steenbergen C., et al., *The Polder Atlas of the Netherlands* (Bussum: Thoth Publishers, 2009), 490; Fan Z., "Research on the Water Conservancy of South of the Yangtze River and Western Zhejiang," in Zheng Z. (ed.), *Water Technology History of Lake Tai* (Beijing, China Agriculture Press, 1980), 264.
2. Li H., *History of Shaoxing in the Qianlong Period* (Shanghai, Shanghai Bookstore Publishing House, 1993), 18.

# Beautiful Countryside
# 美丽乡村


**张晋石 | ZHANG Jinshi**

Associate Professor and master tutor, School of Landscape Architecture, Beijing Forestry University. Zhang is also a contributing editor of *Chinese Landscape Architecture Journal* and *Landscape Architecture Journal*. His research interests lie in landscape architecture and urbanization, and rural landscape. He has published more than 25 articles and has directed over 30 projects. He is the author of *The Significance of Rural Landscape in Landscape Architecture* and *Roberto Burle Marx*.

北京林业大学园林学院副教授、硕士生导师。《中国园林》杂志特约编辑，《风景园林》杂志特约编辑。主要从事风景园林规划与设计、风景园林历史与理论的研究和教学工作。研究兴趣为风景园林与城市化、乡村景观。发表文章25余篇，主持和参与风景园林实践项目30余项。出版著作《乡村景观在风景园林中的意义》与《西方现代风景园林设计师丛书——布雷·马克斯》。


China is an agricultural country. In its long history, hundreds of millions of farmers have worked and lived their lives in the fields and villages. They not only provide us with the material conditions for our survival, but also create a beautiful rural environment. The Chinese people's understanding of the aesthetics of the rural landscape is deep and old. In the *Book of Songs* (11th to 7th century BCE) and *Chuci* (2nd century BCE), there are verses that praise the scenery of the fields. Tao Yuanming, the pioneer of idyllic poetry during the Wei, Jin, and Southern and Northern Dynasties, created a simple and natural pastoral concept in his poem *Returning to My Farm* and also painted beautiful rural scenery. A small straw house hidden among the trees with distant villages is a common image and one that resonates through the ages in China.

Since the Tang Dynasty, a large number of outstanding poets have described the rural landscape as idyllic. This pastoral aesthetic has also influenced the artistic creation of Chinese classical gardens. In the country manor before the Tang and Song Dynasties, the owner of the garden lived in the natural landscape and built their residence by reference to natural and rural conditions. In the mature period of the garden, the natural and the rural landscape was represented by scenes and idyllic spots in the private gardens, reflecting the owner's attachment to the rural life; indeed, the royal gardens established fruit gardens and straw houses to create rural style sceneries. With

河北邯郸乡村景观

Typical rural landscape in Handan, Hebei Province

this faux agricultural landscape, the emperor could parade his concern for farming, which was, at the time, the basis of power.

To understand the rural landscape from a scientific perspective, we believe that the rural landscape is formed in a certain historical period by people who managed their land under the influence of various social, economic, technological, and other comprehensive factors. As a typical cultural landscape, the rural landscape thus embodies and preserves the texture of adaptation formed over thousands of years of interaction between humans and nature, recording the evolution of human society and allowing people to understand previous cultures, farming techniques, and rural lifestyles.

Today, rural land occupies most of China's territory and is home to around 560 million people. The rural landscapes of different regions and different cultures have their own characteristics, showing the diversity of the national landscape. As a basic production space, the rural landscapes

中国是一个农业大国，在漫长的历史过程中，亿万农民在田野、村落中劳作生息。他们不仅为人类提供了赖以生存的物质条件，同时也创造了乡村环境的美。中国人对乡村景观的审美的认识是很早的，在《诗经》和《楚辞》中就有赞美田野风光的诗句。魏晋南北朝时期的陶渊明是田园诗的开创者，在他的《归田园居》中，描绘了优美的乡村风光和田园景象，创造了纯朴自然的田园意境。方宅草屋，树木掩映、远村如烟、鸡鸣犬吠——最平常的村居景象，充满了勃勃生机，成为一个和平宁静的世外桃源。

唐以后，大批优秀的田园诗人创造了大量的诗歌作品，这些作品赋予乡村景观田园般的诗情画意。这样的田园审美影响到了中国古典园林的艺术创作。在唐宋以前的郊野庄园中，古人居于山水之间，利用自然条件营建居所和游憩设施，其中的田园风光也成为庄园的重要组成内容，兼具经济性和欣赏性的作用。到了园林的成熟期，之前庄园环境中的乡村田园景观转化为私家花园中具有田园意境的景点，反映了园主人对乡村生活的眷恋；皇家园林中开辟蔬圃果园、设茅屋草舍而形成的乡村田园式景点，标榜了在这个以农为本的帝国中，帝王对农事的关心。

今天，我们以科学的眼光来认识乡村景观，认为乡村景观是在一定的历史时期内，生活在乡村地区的人们在各种社会、经济、技术等多种综合因素的作用下，经营着所生活的土地而形成的，是人与自然相互适应而产生的"自然的"结果。作为典型的文化景观，乡村景观保留着几千年来人与自然相互作用过程中而形成的肌理，记录着人类社会的演变，可以让人们了解以前的文化、技术和生活方式。

在中国目前，约有5.6亿人生活在农村，作为重要的生活空间，为人类提供多样的生活方式和生存的环境。不同地域、不同文化的乡村景观各具特色，展示着国土景观的多样性。乡村作为基本的生产空间，提供了粮食生产和重要农产品供给；相对城市区域而言，乡村区域与生态关系更加密切，提供了野生动植物的栖息地，为城市提供生态安全屏障。

在全球化、现代化和城市化发展的进程中，中国历史上长期稳定的乡村景观面临着一些威胁，乡村景观承受着巨大的压力以满足各种城市化发展的需求。资源开发、不明智的农业做法、基础设施和乡村地区的工业发展造成乡村景观特殊品质的退化或丧失，对传统乡村风貌、区域生态环境以及一些历史遗迹产生了冲击，对乡村景观的美学价值、自然过程造成了严重的伤害。

乡村景观是一个有限的、日益减少的资源，它们的保护、保存和维护对国家福祉非常重要。为子孙后代的利益保存这些资产只能通过合理的原则、政策和做法，包括明智的土地利用规划、设计和管理来实现。进入21世纪，一系列关于乡村的政策出台，其中一些达到了国家战略的层面。2002年，城乡统筹建设正式拉开帷幕；2005，提出建设社会主义新农村的目标；2014年提出要建设各具特色的美丽乡村，并发布美丽乡村建设十大模式，为中国的美丽乡村建设提供范本和借鉴；2017年提出乡村振兴战略，涉及经济、社会、景观、文化等多方面要素，为乡村景观可持续发展提供了历史性机遇。

乡村面积广袤，既有山水林田湖草等自然资源，又有村落屋舍乡风民俗等人文资源；既包括宏观尺度的自然景观和农耕景观，也包括微观尺度的村落聚落景观，是一个复杂的综合系统。乡村景观的管理、维护和

provide grain and other important agricultural products. Compared with urban areas, rural areas are more closely related to ecology, providing habitats for wildlife and ecological security buffers for cities. The protection and promotion of rural landscapes is crucial to maintaining cultural diversity and biodiversity in China.

In the process of globalization, modernization, and urbanization, the rural landscape that has long been stable in Chinese history is under tremendous pressure. Resource exploitation, unwise agricultural practices, urban sprawl, infrastructure construction, and industrial development in rural areas have caused the degradation of the ecological and aesthetic qualities of rural landscapes.

Rural landscape is a limited and declining resource, and its protection, preservation, and maintenance are very important to national well-being. Preserving these assets for the benefit of future generations can only be achieved through sound principles, policies, and practices. Since entering the 21st century, China has introduced a series of policies on rural development, some of which have reached the level of national strategies. In 2002, the urban and rural overall planning construction officially began; in 2005, the goal of building a new socialist countryside was proposed; in 2014, it was proposed to build a "beautiful countryside" with unique characteristics, and the ten models of beautiful rural construction were released to provide models and references for construction; and in 2017, the rural revitalization strategy was proposed. This last is a national strategy involving economic, social, landscape, cultural, and other factors, providing a historic opportunity for the sustainable development of rural landscapes.

The rural area is vast, with natural resources such as mountains, rivers, forests, farmlands, lakes grasslands, and human resources such as village houses and folk customs. It includes both natural and agricultural landscapes at the macro scale, as well as village settlements at the micro scale. It is a complex integrated system. The management, maintenance, and design of rural landscapes involves the natural sciences (such as hydrology, forestry, soil, agriculture), the humanities (such as cultural landscapes, semiotics, sociology), and applied sciences (such as landscape architecture, architecture, planning). It involves a number of management departments with clear divisions such as planning, forestry, agriculture, and water conservancy; it also involves policy-makers, designers, and the main creators of rural landscapes – farmers who live and work on the land.

To achieve sensible and sustainable land use, planning, design, and management in rural areas, the most important values for rural landscapes should be understanding and respect. The texture of the rural landscape is composed of various plots—fields, grasslands, woodlands, rivers, country roads, terraces, wetlands, villages—each presenting a unique form of landscape structure. These unique landscape structures and forms are the basis for understanding the history, function, and ecology of a village, and then managing, maintaining, and designing rural landscapes. The sustainable development of the village must take these characteristics into account. Understanding and respecting the landscape structure can help us cope with the simplification caused by globalization, and protect and reveal them as the core characteristics of the cultural landscape and the most important values in future design.

The rural landscape that has been shaped over thousands of years in China is our most important resource. It not only accumulates knowledge about environmental sustainability, but also embodies values of production, ecology, identity, and heritage. Everyone must do their best to protect the quality of this common wealth.

设计涉及到自然科学(如水文、森林、土壤、农业)、人文科学(如文化景观、符号学、社会学等)以及应用科学(如风景园林、建筑和规划等);涉及到规划、林业、农业、水利等分工明确的多个管理部门;涉及到政策制定者、设计师、以及乡村景观的主要创造者——生活工作在这个土地上的农民。

对于乡村景观的最主要价值观应该是"理解与尊重"。乡村景观的肌理由各种地块所组成:田野、草原、林地、河流、乡间小路、梯田、湿地、村庄等等,呈现出独特的景观结构形式。这些独特的景观结构和形式是了解一处乡村的历史、功能、生态,进而进行乡村景观管理、维护和设计的基础,乡村的可持续发展必须要将基地的历史与这些特征纳入考虑。对景观结构的理解和尊重能够帮助我们面对全球化过程所造成的单一化现象,理解并保护基地的特征、并在未来的设计中进行保留和显露是最重要的价值观。

乡村景观经历长时间的塑造,已经成为我们最重要的资源。它不仅积累了创造可持续环境的知识,也具有生产、生态、环境、识别和遗产等多元价值,每一个人都必须尽力来保护这份共同财富的品质。

# Building Beautiful China: Rural Case Studies
# 建设美丽中国：美丽乡村案例研究

**张天洁 | ZHANG Tianjie**

Professor, School of Architecture, Tianjin University. Zhang is also deputy director of Tianjin University's Center for International Affairs, and of the Institute of Urban Heritage Preservation and Regeneration. Zhang's teaching and research interests include transcultural landscape, heritage preservation and cultural tourism, rural revitalization, spatial performance, and justice. She has published widely on these subjects, and has given over 30 guest lectures in Asia and North America.

天津大学建筑学院教授、国际交流部副主任、城市历史保护与发展研究所副所长。主要研究领域为跨文化景观、遗产保护、地方创生等。曾在中国核心刊物与英文书籍中广泛发表相关主题的论文，应邀在美、澳、新加坡、日等国际会议作专题发言30余次。曾获美国亚洲研究国际奖金、美国建筑史学会国际奖金、新加坡亚研所国际奖金。

When visiting Zhoushan, Zhejiang Province in 2015, President Xi Jinping said, "To build a beautiful China, we must ensure the construction of beautiful countryside. Only by building new countryside with distinctive characteristics can we build a beautiful China with rich connotations."[1] Building a beautiful China is a grand goal. Beautiful countryside is not only the foundation and premise of building a beautiful China, but also the means to realize the ideal of an ecological civilization.[2]

The slogan "beautiful countryside" can be traced back to 2008. The government of Anji County, Zhejiang Province was the first to propose building a beautiful countryside. In 2010, the successful experience of Anji County was officially promoted throughout Zhejiang Province. In 2013, China's Ministry of Finance launched the national project of building beautiful countryside, offering awards and subsidies for pilot projects. Accordingly, a nationwide movement of making beautiful countryside has ensued. Beautiful countryside involves multiple objectives, such as renovating abandoned villages, reconstructing rural space, improving rural standards of living, narrowing the rural–urban income gap, and promoting rural-urban integrated development.

Building a beautiful countryside is just the latest phase in the constant transformation and development of China's rural areas by the central

大淀头沿河街道景观
Waterfront streetscape in Dadiantou Village

government. Since the middle of the 20th century, China's rural areas have experienced profound change, as evidenced by the household responsibility system (a policy that each household should be responsible for the quantity and quality of their own production), township and village enterprises, non-agriculturalization (which frees rural people to work in cities or in non-farming jobs), dysfunction of local administrations, and rural labor migration. The corresponding industrialization and urbanization of peri-urban and rural lands has rapidly altered the physical and cultural aspects of the rural landscape.[3] The rapid industrialization and urbanization process has driven significant changes in the core elements of rural development: land, capital, and labor.[4]

Beautiful countryside construction projects have received support from the government in terms of both policy and funding. This has significantly improved the rural living environment and has inspired some to return to the countryside. Beautifying China's rural landscape has captured the imagination of government, elites, and the public. Capital

2015年，习近平总书记考察美丽浙江建设，指出："中国要美，乡村必须美。建设各具特色的新农村，才会有千姿百态的美丽中国，美丽中国需要这种人人向往的乡愁圣地、风情家园"[1]。建设美丽中国是我们的宏伟目标，其重点和难点都在乡村。美丽乡村既是美丽中国建设的基础和前提，也是推进生态文明和新农村建设的新工程、新载体[2]。

"美丽乡村"这一说法，可以追溯至2008年浙江省安吉县立足县情开始"中国美丽乡村建设"。2010年浙江省全面推广安吉经验。2013年国家财政部采取一事一议奖补方式在全国启动美丽乡村建设试点。中国掀起了美丽乡村建设的新热潮，旨在解决空心村整治、乡村空间重构、人居环境改善、城乡差距缩小和城乡一体化等诸多议题。

美丽乡村建设实质上是中国乡村转型发展中的一环，是中央政府干预乡村发展的系列战略性引导政策之一。自20世纪中叶以来，中国乡村发生了深刻的变革，责任制，乡镇企业，非农化、机能失调，乡村劳动力迁移变革引发的工业化和城市化急剧改变了我国乡村的物质和人文景观[3]。而1980年代以来的快速工业化和城镇化进程，驱使以土地、资金和劳动力为核心的乡村发展要素发生重大变化，引发乡村地域的生产、生活、生态和文化功能逐渐演变，进而导致了乡村的重构。独特的城乡二元结构及快速的城乡经济社会发展进程，使得中国的乡村重构具有丰富的内涵[4]。

美丽乡村项目携带着大量的公共财政资源，显著改善了乡村人居环境，提升了乡村治理的效能，亦深刻改变了乡村治理的利益格局。实际上，在建设美丽乡村的国策下，回归乡村、找寻"乡村"成为了政府、精英人士、社会大众的共同取向。同时，产品下乡、资本下乡成为新时期实现资本升值的一种选择。在此背景下，美丽乡村的推动主体越来越多元。按照投资主体不同，美丽乡村建设可以大体分为政府主导型、资本主导型和农户自主型三种模式[5]。

政府主导型的一个案例是河北省安新县大淀头村[6]。地处京津冀地区重要的生态屏障白洋淀，大淀头村于2013年入选河北省美丽乡村建设示范的重点村，由各级地方政府共同推进了美丽乡村规划和建设。地方政府运用增减挂钩政策，推动农民集中居住，并调动民间资本投资乡村建设。重点工作包括：整治环境卫生，垃圾收运、污水处理，改善生态环境；完善公共服务设施配套；保护原生绿化水体景观风貌、分片引导建筑风貌。努力打造白洋淀"天蓝、水清、苇绿、荷红、村美、人幸福"的北国水乡风韵，建成美丽乡村的示范区[7]。

资本主导型的一个案例是天津蓟州渔阳镇西井峪村。它是天津唯一的国家级历史文化名村，2009年编制完成保护规划，但在村集体主导下，该方案难以落地。全村常住人口持续下降，人均年收入增长乏力，村落风貌日渐衰败。渔阳镇政府持续关注了保护规划实施成效欠佳的问题，于2015年同北京九略旅游管理公司签订了西井峪乡村旅游项目全程委托运营服务合同。九略驻村工作3年，围绕农业、农村、村民等开展了多项规划设计和运营实践，得到了游客和村民的广泛认可。以"农村"为招牌，建设优美的乡村环境，吸引游客关注；以"农业"为核心，对内提高农民收入，对外向城市输出"乡村"概念；以"村民"是根基，在村民中重塑文化共同体，改变村民只重短期经济利益的价值

investment in the countryside has also become diversified. According to the different investment actors, three types of construction can be identified: government-guided, capital-guided, and villagers-guided.[5]

One example of government-guided construction is Dadiantou Village in Anxin County, Hebei Province.[6] The village is located in Baiyangdian, which is an important wetland and ecological barrier in the Beijing-Tianjin-Hebei region. In 2013, it was selected as a key pilot project of beautiful countryside construction in Hebei Province. Local governments at all levels jointly promoted the plan. Adopting the policy of "linking up increased urban construction land with decreased rural construction land," the government promoted investment in waste management, sewage treatment, ecological improvement, public services, and landscape heritage, as well as creating guidelines regarding architectural styles. The government made great efforts to turn Dadiantou Village into a water town with "blue sky, clear water, green dragonfly, red lotus, beautiful scenery, and happy villagers." The result is that Dadiantou is now a demonstration area for the creation of beautiful countryside in Hebei Province.[7]

An example of capital-guided construction is Xijingyu Village in Yuyang Town, Jizhou District, Tianjin. Xijingyu Village is the only National Historical and Cultural Village in Tianjin. The preservation plan for the village was completed in 2009; however, under the leadership of the village collective, the plan was hard to implement. The village faced many problems, such as decreasing population, the slow growth of per capita income, and the gradual erosion of traditional character. Yuyang Town government noticed the difficulties of plan implementation, and in 2015 contracted with the Jiulüe Tourism Management Company (Jiulüe) to achieve a beautiful countryside tourism project in Xijingyu. Jiulüe stayed in Xijingyu for three years, and carried out a series of planning and design operations focusing on agriculture, countryside, and villages. Their work has been widely appreciated by tourists and villagers. Firstly, "countryside" was considered as a brand, so a beautiful countryside environment was built up to attract

西井峪石磨小品

Millstone in historic Xijingyu Village

tourists. Secondly, "agriculture" was considered as the core, so it was developed to raise farmers' income and at the same time export the concept of "rural area" to the city. Thirdly, "villages" were recognized as the foundation, therefore a cultural community was rebuilt among villagers and their value orientation toward short-term economic benefit was changed. The villagers in Xijingyu started to understand, support, accept, and participate in the project. The beautiful countryside construction in Xijingyu has moved from a traditional top-down project to a participatory multiple-stakeholder project. As an external actor, Jiulüe has helped in activating the participation of villagers and guiding the village from the difficult times of gradual decline to a path toward sustainable development.[8]

A successful case of villagers-guided construction can be found in Yanhe Village, Gucheng County in the southwestern mountainous area of Hubei Province. Without government funds or special resource advantages, the beautiful countryside construction was led autonomously by the local village committee. Green Cross, a non-governmental environmental

取向，让村民理解、支持、接受和参与。西井峪的美丽乡村建设经历了从传统自上而下到多元主体参与的转变。九略作为民间的外在助力之一，协助调动村民参与，帮助该村从日渐衰败的困局逐渐步入可持续发展之路[8]。

农户自主型的一个案例是湖北省西南山区谷城县堰河村。该村没有依靠政府资金扶助或特殊的资源优势，而是以村支两委为主导，公益性环保组织绿十字提供建议指导，村民和企业广泛参与，把昔日污水横流垃圾遍地的村落建设成为了"中国最美休闲乡村"。堰河村一改"蓝图式规划"模式，而采用行动式规划，有效应对了乡村空间资源配置逻辑由"关系"[9]向"社会资本"的转型。首先，从关系村民生活的小事——垃圾分类入手，发动广泛的村民参与。第二，依靠本地资源，建立立体综合的茶园种植模式，引入旅游开发、手工艺品生产、农产品外销等手段丰富产业形式，提高村民收入。第三，挖掘本地文化，开办多样化的活动，塑造地方认同，丰富村民精神世界。在行动中充分调动参与者热情，提升了社会信任，形成规范、增强关系网络，有效地培育了社会资本，实现了美丽乡村和可持续发展[10]。

总体而言，美丽乡村重在共建、共享、共治。在多元主体参与的新模式下，如何确保农户福利增进？如何做好本地社区的赋能培育？如何确保乡村公共产品的长期稳定供给？如何调动民间资本参与的积极性？如何发挥和协调政府、村民的内在动力和民间的外在助力实现村庄稳健治理和可持续发展？如何实现乡村物质环境和社会经济文化层面的多重重构与复兴？这些问题都有待我们进一步解答。让我们共同努力共同期待美丽乡村的美好明天。

protection organization, was asked to provide suggestions and help. Villagers and enterprises participated extensively in the construction and together they turned "the village with wastewater and garbage everywhere" into "the most beautiful leisure village in China." Instead of using a "blueprint plan," Yanhe adopted an action plan, which effectively responded to the transformation from *guanxi*[9] to "social capital" in rural spatial resource allocation logic. The construction started with small issues in village life, such as garbage classification, to encourage the participation of residents. Then, relying on local resources, the village established a tea planting program. By means of tourism development, handicraft production, and agricultural products, the villagers' income has been greatly increased. Finally, Yanhe paid attention to its local culture. Diversified cultural activities were instigated, local identity was reshaped, and the spiritual world of villagers has consequently been enriched. During the construction, the enthusiasm of participants was mobilized and trust was developed. The action plan of Yanhe Village has effectively cultivated social capital and achieved the sustainable development of beautiful countryside.[10]

There are many questions we need to focus on as we work together to build beautiful countryside. Under the new mode of multiple stakeholders, how can we guarantee the increase of villagers' well-being? How can we engage and empower local communities? How can we ensure the stable supply of rural public goods? How can we encourage private investment? How can we coordinate the internal power from local government and villagers with external power so as to achieve effective governance and sustainable development? And how can we accomplish the multidimensional reconstruction and revitalization of rural areas in the physical environment, as well as the social, economic, and cultural aspects? All these questions need to be explored further. Let's work together and look forward to the beautiful future of beautiful countryside in China.

1. Zhejiang Daily, "Beautiful China Depends on the Beautiful Countryside," (May 25, 2017) http://zjrb.zjol.com.cn/html/2017-05/25/content_3054319.htm?div=-1.
2. Liu Y., Zhou Y., "Challenges and Countermeasures for the Construction of Beautiful Rural Areas in China," *Journal of Agricultural Resources and Environment* 2 (2015): 97–105.
3. Long H., et al., "Building New Countryside in China: A geographical perspective," *Land Use Policy* 27, no. 2 (2010): 470.
4. Long H., et al., "The Allocation and Management of Critical Resources in Rural China Under Restructuring: Problems and prospects," *Journal of Rural Studies* 47 (2016): 392–412.
5. Yao S. & Long T., "A Comparative Study on the Modes of Beautiful Villages Construction from the Perspective of Improving Villagers' Wellbeing," *Journal of Sichuan University (Philosophy and Social Sciences)* 1 (2019): 170–80.
6. Baiyangdian, where the village is located, is the largest freshwater lake in North China and plays an important role in maintaining the balance of wetland ecosystems in the Beijing-Tianjin-Hebei region, replenishing groundwater and protecting biodiversity. In 2017, it was included in the Xiong'an New District.
7. Yang Y. & Zhang T., "Remaking a Jiangnan in Northern China: An Investigation on the Beautiful Village Project in Anxin County, Hebei Province," paper presented at IUSAM (2017).
8. Zhang T., Zhang L. & Yang Y., "An Exploration on the Implementation of Traditional Village Conservation with Enterprise Involvement: A Case Study of Xijingyu Village, Jixian County, Tianjin," *China City Planning Review* (2018) 42–48.
9. *Guanxi*, which usually refers to the relationship between acquaintances, has been the basis of social interaction in traditional agricultural societies in China for thousands of years.
10. Xu Q. & Zhang T., "Revitalizing China's Countryside with NGO's Participation: A Case Study of Yanhe Village, Hubei Province, China," paper presented at the Great Asian Streets Symposium (2018).

# XL Greenhouse
# 大棚景观

韩涛 | HAN Tao

Professor and Director of the graduate program, School of Architecture, Central Academy of Fine Arts. Han is also Deputy Secretary General of the Chinese Artists Association's Committee of Architectural Art, founder of the Beijing-based institute THANLAB, and has been a visiting scholar at Columbia University's Graduate School of Architecture, Planning, and Preservation. His works such as *Cultural Worker, The Form for Community, Future Consumption Spaces, Chinese Academy of Oil Painting, and 798 2010 Art Space* have been widely published and have featured in biennales both domestic and abroad.

中央美院建筑学院教授、研究生部主任中国美术家协会建筑艺术委员会副秘书长,哥伦比亚大学访问学者,以北京为基地的THANLAB(装置研究所)的创立者与学术主持。他的"文化工人"、"共同体的形式"与"未来消费空间","中国油画院"、"798 2010艺术空间" 等多个项目被广泛出版及参加国内外多个双年展。

Today, the Chinese countryside is not an idyllic landscape. Instead, it is more likely to feature vast areas of continuous plastic greenhouses. In Shouguang, Shandong Province, and in Kunming, Yunnan Province, hundreds of villages have been connected by the ocean-like surface of the greenhouses forming an archipelago in a plastic ocean. The reality of the Chinese countryside that we are facing today is no longer the pictorial imagination of the pre-modern legacy, but the expression of modernization and with it the extinction of the traditional village. Agricultural peasants now become assembly-line workers in plastic factories and the rural landscape becomes an object of capital consumption. A critical appreciation of these realities is the prerequisite for a true understanding of Beautiful China.

With the rise of modernity and the mass production of glass, the greenhouse emerged as an incubator of scientific experiments and an icon of the worldwide collection system of colonialism. After the 18th century, the greenhouse served as a botanical and zoological exhibition space in aristocratic and eventually public urban settings. In the 19th century, the greenhouse was used to showcase capitalist commodities reaching its apotheosis in the form of the Crystal Palace in London's Hyde Park in 1851. By the middle of the 20th century, the invention of plastics enabled the

creation of the XL greenhouse (*dapeng* in Chinese) and they have since covered vast tracts of not only China's agricultural landscape, but the world's.

My recent research has focused on the XL greenhouse as an architectural icon of late modernity. Whilst clearly an architectural typology, the XL greenhouse is also a landscape architectural phenomenon, one that opens up discourse about Beautiful China and contemporary design. Architecturally the XL greenhouse is not about quality, only quantity. The XL greenhouse is an extreme version of Fordism – through the repetition and spread of the homogeneous grid, it transforms the land in the most economical and temporary way. The diversity and variability of nature, terrain, ecology, land, climate, and air have been removed and replaced by streamlined agricultural production and profit accumulation. If capitalism is essentially not an economy of quality but an economy of quantity, the XL greenhouses represent the absolute form of capitalist production. When combined with contemporary big data and digital surveillance

今天的中国的乡村并非总是沉浸在一片田园风光中，更多情况下，包裹它们的，可能是连绵成片的塑料大棚。在山东寿光与云南昆明，数以百计的乡村已经全被海洋状的大棚连接起来。我们今天面对的中国乡村现实，已经不再是前现代遗存的画境式想象，而是现代化进程的完成，是传统乡村的灭绝。农民成为计时工人，原始农业成为农业产业，乡村景观成为资本消费对象，乡村成为国家生命政治的治理工具。如何批判性理解这些现实，是批判性理解“美丽中国”运动的前提。

随着现代性的兴起与玻璃的发明，温室进入了科学家工作的实验场所，同时作为世界的收集场所进入了绝对君权的殖民化景观收藏展示系统。18世纪之后，温室作为一种主题公园模式贵族社会与城市广为扩散。19世纪，温室技术则在伦敦海德公园以水晶宫的极端形式，进入到了资本主义世界商品展示系统。到了20世纪中期，塑料的发明使得大棚开始登上了历史舞台。20世纪中期，大棚不仅大规模地覆盖了中国的农业景观，也覆盖了世界。

我的研究将大棚作为后现代的建筑反传统图腾。它很显然是一个建筑类型的同时，也是一个景观现象，这

个现象开启了美丽中国与当代设计的探讨论述。大棚是一种没有质量，只有数量的建筑学。大棚是福特制工厂形式逻辑的极端版本——通过均质网格的重复与蔓延，以最经济、最轻、最临时的方式，参与了土地的改造。在绝对形式与内容的双重格式化下，自然、地形、生态、土地、气候、空气的多样性与变化性已经被去除。如果资本主义本质上不是一种关于质量的经济，而是关于数量的经济，那么，大棚就是资本主义生产的绝对形式。当大棚与当代大数据和数字监控技术相结合时，无处不在的大棚似乎成了现代性的终极反乌托邦。

如果大棚已经成为美丽乡村运动中不可被回避的客观现实，我的设计研究探索了这个中性框架的内部的潜力，这种潜力并非仅仅服务于农业生产，而是充满了重新内容化的无限可能性。例如，大棚的室内空间可以方便各种形式的社交聚会、节日庆典、艺术作品、表演、娱乐、纪念缅怀，甚至可以作为包含了历史景观痕迹的复写本。

我们在在北京城乡结合部的一处大棚中，我和我的学生们就发现了这样一个潜能性的案例。我们发现了一处处于大棚海洋中半透明小屋。开始以为这是对现有树

technology, a landscape of ubiquitous XL greenhouses appears as modernity's ultimate dystopia.

If the ubiquity of the XL greenhouse has become an objective reality that cannot be avoided, my design research has explored the potential for the interior of this neutral framework to not only serve agricultural production, but also offer possibilities for partial reprogramming. For example, the interior spaces could facilitate various forms of social gathering, festival celebrations, artistic works, performances, recreation, memorials, and even include traces of the historical landscape palimpsest.

Exploring XL greenhouses in the peri-urban area of Beijing, my students and I have discovered evidence of such alternative uses. We have even found a translucent hut, which at first we thought to be a protective membrane for existing trees but upon closer inspection was found to be a family cemetery. Even here, in the rootless economic landscape of the post-human era, the most personal memories find a ritualistic locus.

The owner of this XL greenhouse carefully placed his personal memory into the machinery of modern labor, resisting the erasure and simplification of personal traces by the logic of collective land ownership.

This study of XL greenhouses offers several insights relevant to the pursuit of Beautiful China. The first is that modernity will always contain traces of internal difference and resistance. Following this, the second insight is that the application of Beautiful China to the rural landscape is potentially an ideological illusion, signaling the deeper spread of urbanization and rationality into the countryside and that this is only a singular version of Beautiful China. The third insight—or rather, conclusion—is that we might strive to construct a plural Beautiful China wherein Beautiful China is not a singular model of a single subject, nor a nostalgic complex of pre-modern culture, but a transition to post-industrial civilization that shows respect for pre-industrial civilization. This is the inherent essence of Beautiful China.

木的保护性围合，走进之后却发现这是一个家族墓地。我和我的学生在后人类时代的现场，看到了最无根性的经济生产逻辑与最私人化的个人记忆瞬间交织在一起的可能性。这处大棚的主人小心的把自己的私人记忆安放在现代劳动生活的场景之中，抵抗着集体土地所有权逻辑对个人痕迹的抹去、擦除与简化。

大棚的研究为追求美丽中国的梦想提供了一些见解。其一，即使作为现代性最典型特征的大棚，其内部也具有内在差异与内在抵抗的可能性。其二，我们今天所讨论的美丽中国所暗含的城市向乡村的回归，其实是一个国家立场的意识形态假象，其本质是城市化进程向乡村的继续深度扩散。这仅是一个单数版本的美丽中国。其三，我们要努力共同建构一个复数的“美丽中国”。只有这样，当前正在发生的国家立场的“美丽中国”运动，才不能被简化为一种单一主体的固有模式，也不会被简化为面向前现代文化的怀旧情结，而是一个尊重前工业文明、基于工业文明、超越工业文明、面向未来多主体杂交的后工业文化转向实践。这才是“美丽中国”所应具有的内在本质。

# The Beauty of Brownfield Regeneration
# 棕地之美

**郑晓笛 | ZHENG Xiaodi**

Associate Professor and Vice Chair, Department of Landscape Architecture, School of Architecture, Tsinghua University. Zheng serves as General-Secretary of the Chinese Steering Committee of Landscape Architecture Education and is the official delegate of the Chinese Society of Landscape Architecture at the International Federation of Landscape Architects Asia-Pacific Region council. Her current research focuses on brownfields regeneration and sustainable landscapes, as well as campus landscape planning and design. She has published a number of papers in Chinese and English professional journals and is recipient of the 2017 Council of Education in Landscape Architecture President's Award.

清华大学建筑学院副教授，景观学系副系主任。美国注册风景园林师、美国风景园林师协会会员、中国风景园林协会会员。现任2018－2022年教育部高等学校建筑类专业教学指导委员会风景园林专业教学指导分委员会秘书长、国际风景园林师联合会亚太区（IFLA APR）中国代表。主要研究方向为城市棕地与废弃地改造再生、校园景观设计研究、风景园林设计理论。在多个国内外专业期刊发表论文10余篇。获2017年（国际）风景园林教育者联合会（CELA）主席奖。

What is the public perception of environmental issues in China? In 2017 Ipsos, the world's third-largest market research company, conducted a survey titled "What Worries the World" in which randomly selected respondents were asked to list the most worrying problems in their own countries. Of the countries surveyed, only China listed environmental issues as the biggest common concern.

Brownfield regeneration has become a hot subject in China in recent years. At present, the three main types of brownfield under transformation are idle industrial and infrastructural land, mining wasteland, and landfill. Driven by the policy of ecological civilization and Beautiful China, China has taken a series of measures to facilitate contamination remediation. In 2014, the government released the National Soil Pollution Survey Report to the public; in 2016, the release of the 10-chapter Action Plan for Soil Pollution Prevention and Control greatly promoted the treatment of soil contamination; in 2017, the City Betterment and Ecological Restoration Programs were related to brownfields, and finally, the Soil Pollution Prevention and Control Law, providing a legal basis for China's soil pollution control, was implemented on January 1, 2019.

A number of NGOs have begun to investigate the environmental threat of contaminated sites in China, but the details remain unclear and in-depth

investigation of soil pollution is ongoing work typically being carried out by provincial governments. On the other hand, there are as many as 36 government ministries and commissions listed in Action Plan for Soil Pollution Prevention and Control, so how to encourage cooperation among these ministries and implement regeneration projects are some of the many challenges we are facing. These challenges notwithstanding, China has rapidly completed a series of large-scale exemplary brownfield regeneration projects under huge development pressure, transforming derelict sites into "beautiful" parks and open spaces. This brownfield regeneration surge is both encouraging and alarming. Is becoming beautiful the end goal for brownfield regeneration? What is beauty in this context, and how do we make beauty through landscape practice?

Recently, as guest editor for the February 2019 issue of *Chinese Landscape Architecture* with the theme of brownfield restoration and design, I put forward two main areas for research regarding brownfields. The first is "vision," which calls for a synthetic understanding of

在中国，公众对于环境问题的认知是怎样的呢？2017年全球第三大机构Ipsos进行了一次名为"What Worries the World（什么让世界担忧）"的调研，即从全世界选中的国家中随机抽取民众，让他们列出自己国家中最令人担忧的问题。其中，中国所列出的问题就是对于"环境的威胁"。在被调研的众多国家里，只有中国将环境问题列为最令他们担忧的且需要共同面对的问题。

过去的几年中，棕地修复已经成为了中国的热门研究主题。目前，中国正处于修复改造的最主要的三类棕地包括工业与基础设施闲置地、采矿业废弃地和垃圾填埋场。在生态文明和美丽中国的政策推动下，中国采取了一系列的措施：2014年，政府向公众公布了《全国土壤污染状况调查公报》；2016年，"土十条"发布，极大推动了土壤污染的治理工作；2017年，城市双修的生态修复和城市修补都与棕地相关；2018年底公布和2019年1月1号正式实施的《土壤污染防治法》，真正的为中国的土壤污染治理提供了法律基础。

中国已经开始出现一些公益组织对污染场地对于公众的威胁进行调研，但是威胁的具体情况到现在为止，依

然并不清晰。因此各个省份的土壤污染详查是一个重要且正进行中的工作。在"土十条"里面涉及到的政府部委多达36个，关于这些部委之间如何协作和在具体的实施中如何操作的问题，也是我们现在所面临的挑战之一。不过即使在这样的挑战与发展压力下，我们也迅速完成了一系列大规模的示范性棕地再生项目，将废弃的场地改造成"美丽"的公园和开放空间。这一棕地更新浪潮既令人鼓舞又令人担忧。"美丽"是棕地改造的最终目标吗?在这种背景下，什么是美?我们又如何在风景园林实践过程中来创造美?

在我们风景园林的研究领域内，可以看到近些年棕地类的研究呈现上升趋势。我们探讨的项目里，有近乎一半的项目是工业基础设施闲置地一类的场地。最近，在我协助组织的以棕地修复与设计为主题的《中国园林》2019年第二期的刊首语中，我提出了两个建议，同时也是我的课题组目前主要推进的方向。其一是"vision(眼界)"。我们需要以一个更大、更区域的视角看待棕地问题。它需要我们综合理解棕地再生之美，无论是在数量上还是在规模上。这种美不仅仅是审美价值，更重要的是棕地再生所能带来的生态、社会和经济价值。工业自然所提供的丰富而

the beauty of brownfield regeneration both in multitude and in scale. This beauty is not mere aesthetic value, but more importantly ecological, social, and economic value that brownfields regeneration can contribute. The rich and unique habitat that industrial nature provides has become an important type for ecological research and preservation. Environmental justice is a critical achievement toward building an equal society especially through empowering underprivileged groups impacted by contaminated sites. The land value increase of surrounding blocks and the new investment attracted by turning brownfield sites into beautiful parks are making economically thriving neighborhoods.

In terms of visioning in scale, brownfields are often not just singular sites but networks of sites forming large-scale, contiguous brownfield zones (referred to in my research as "brownfield-clusters"). Driven by land-use policies, China's brownfield-clusters have been amalgamated over a short period of time and often transformed under the same impetus. This provides an opportunity for us to use them to build new urban green space networks as was successfully achieved in Emscher Park in the Ruhr region of Germany.

The second research area is "action." Brownfield regeneration is a highly complex and dynamic process. The concept of "Brown Earth-Work," which emphasizes the physical and spatial dimensions of contamination in brownfield sites, was proposed in my doctoral dissertation completed in 2014. It highlights the need to identify the core element of brownfields and to provide a basis for more effective and efficient collaboration between site remediation professionals (such as environmental engineers) and landscape design professionals. Such collaboration should be conducted as early as possible in the process of brownfield regeneration, which will lead not only to choosing the most efficient remediation strategy, but also to providing more possibilities for the creation of beauty in brownfields.

In 2016, Tsinghua University held the first International Conference on Brownfield Regeneration & Ecological Restoration and we invited scholars and experts from multiple countries, disciplines, and government agencies to exchange ideas. In 2018, the second International Conference was combined with the Chinese Sustainable Environmental Restoration Conference, organized by the China Association of Environmental Protection Industry. In these fora, the discussion of making beauty through brownfield regeneration was opened to a much broader audience including not only landscape architects and urban designers, but also environmental engineers, investors, and government officials. In 2019, the Center for Brownfields Research was established in the School of Architecture at Tsinghua University, with me and Niall Kirkwood from Harvard University acting as joint directors, aiming to provide a transdisciplinary international research and practice platform.

For future generations of landscape architecture academics and practitioners in China, the complexity and scale of brownfield regeneration would be a major challenge that

独特的生境已成为生态研究和保护的重要类型。环境资源平等是建设平等社会的一项重要成就，特别是通过赋予受污染场地影响的贫困群体权力。将棕地改造成美丽公园给周边街区的土地价值增加，以及所吸引的新投资，正在打造经济繁荣型社区。

就"vision（眼界）"中的规模而言，棕地通常不只是单一的场地，而是大型连续棕地区域的成片场地网络(在我的研究中称为"棕地群")。在土地利用政策的推动下，中国的棕地群在很短的时间内进行了合并，并经常在同一动力下发生转变。这为我们提供了一个机会，利用它们来构建新的城市绿地网络系统，德国鲁尔地区的Emscher公园就是一个成功的范例。

其二是"action（行动）"。棕地问题非常复杂，要求高度的跨学科协作，尤其是与环境工程的土壤污染修复专业。2016年，清华大学举办了第一届"棕地再生与生态修复国际会议"，我们邀请到了来自多个国家，多个专业，多个部委的学者和专家对于这个问题进行探讨。2018年，我们所组织的第二届棕地会议相对于第一届来说更往前迈进了一步。因为会议与中国环保产业协会所组织的第二届"中国可持续环境修复大会"相结合，所以关于棕地的风景园林方向的探讨可以面向更多环境修复的工程人员并展开，让两个专业之间的对话和沟通更加的顺畅，风景园林专业人员由此对棕地产生更多的理解，并能参与更多的工作。

2016年，清华大学举办首届棕地再生与生态修复国际研讨会，邀请来自多个国家、学科和政府机构的学者和专家交流意见。2018年，第二届国际会议与中国环保产业协会主办的中国可持续环境恢复大会相结合。在这些论坛上，关于通过棕地改造创造美丽的讨论向更广泛的受众开放，不仅包括风景园林师和城市设计师，还包括环境工程师、投资者和政府官员。清华大学建筑学院棕地研究中心于2019年2月正式成立，哈佛大学的尼尔·柯克伍德教授作为清华大学的杰出访问教授，与我共同作为中心的联合主任，旨在提供一个跨学科的国际研究和实践平台。

对于中国未来几代风景园林学者和从业者来说，棕地更新的复杂性和规模将是他们毕业后需要面对的一个重大挑战。因此，清华大学的课程正在增加新的内容和课

they need to face once they graduate. As such, new content and courses are being added to the curriculum at Tsinghua University to equip them with critical knowledge and methods. Abandoned factory sites, mining wasteland, and closed landfills have become design studio subjects, and students' work has won design awards. In 2018, I initiated the first lecture course on brownfields in China entitled "Theory in Landscape Architecture: Transformative Landscapes," which takes the form of lectures, field trips to brownfield sites, workshops, and seminars to provide a rich and in-depth reading of brownfields to students.

During my work in the field of brownfields regeneration over the past 10 years, I have found that the beauty of it lies in its highly difficult and complex condition which constantly challenges our understanding of the relationship between humankind and nature, questions the core values we hold toward building our future, and calls for more responsible and creative design solutions. Brownfields ask us to think deeply about how we evaluate beauty, the goal and vision of beauty, and the methods by which we create beauty. The challenge is not to just cosmetically beautify brownfield sites, but also to use them as catalysts to improve the ecology and the communities surrounding them.

程，以使他们具备批判性的知识和方法。废弃的厂房、矿山荒地、封闭的垃圾填埋场成为设计工作室的主题，学生的作品获得了设计方面的奖项。2018年，我开设了一门名为“变化之景”的课程，紧密围绕以棕地为契机的景观理论进行探讨；我们不仅设置讲座，并且带学生们去参观棕地改造后的景观项目，也通过workshop（工作坊）的形式，以及研讨会的形式，让大家真实感受并理解到棕色土方以及土壤工程对于场地塑造的作用和意义。

在过去十年所进行的棕地研究过程中，于我而言，它的美在于它非常困难和复杂的条件，这迫使我对于人与自然关系必须进行更深刻的反思与思考，让我思考质疑我们用来建设未来的核心价值观，并开始寻求呼吁更有责任感且更具创意的解决方案。棕地要求我们深入思考我们如何评估定义美，其的目标和愿景，以及我们创造美的方法。我们面临的挑战不仅是美化棕地，还要利用它们作为催化剂，改善棕地周围的生态和社区。

# Toward a Space of Capability
# 走向潜质空间

**朱育帆 | ZHU Yufan**

Deputy Chair, Department of Landscape Architecture, School of Architecture, Tsinghua University and director of ZHU Yufan Studio. Zhu has over 30 publications on design theory, research, and teaching methods. His award-winning design projects include the Quarry Garden in Shanghai Botanical Garden and Shougang Industrial Park in Beijing.

清华大学建筑学院景观学系副系主任。曾发表30余篇与景观设计理论、设计教学与研究方法等相关论文。其主持的多个工程项目均荣获奖项，包括上海辰山植物园矿坑花园、北京首钢工业遗址公园等。

**许愿 | XU Yuan**

Assistant Professor, Department of Landscape Architecture, School of Architecture, Tsinghua University. Xu has received several design awards including the IFLA Zvi Miller Prize (2014). Her recent published research focuses on form-finding in landscape design and Eastern traditional landscape art.

清华大学建筑学院景观学系助理教授。获2014年国际风景园林师联合会学生设计竞赛第二名。主要研究方向为景观设计及其历史与理论，以及设计造型逻辑、空间的场所性、东方传统山水艺术等。

The idea of Beautiful China marks a moment where the rapid urbanization of China is now turning into an era where the quality—not just the scale and speed—of development is a major concern. It is not only an opportunity, but also a challenge for landscape architecture. Maybe landscape architects can see through the re-adaption of the ruins of our times and open what we refer to as "the space of capability." By this we mean the potential of every site to become something new; not entirely new, but something latent within it, drawn to the surface through the act of design – the act of respecting and recognizing a site's potential. This space of capability is also of course a nod to "Capability" Brown, who so famously conjured a naturalistic landscape aesthetic in 18th-century England, and we ask what the equivalent of his achievement might be today? For us, the way into this space of capability—the way into the potential of sites and the potential of our profession—is firstly and most apparently through ruins.

The wonderful book *Hypnerotomachia Poliphili,* first published in 1499, framed and highlighted the aesthetic values of ruins. Three hundred years later, William Gilpin venerated ruins as picturesque aesthetic objects in the English landscape garden. This aesthetic discovery of ruins is profound, because it implied that all the relics of human civilization have the potential and legitimacy for acceptance in a new situation.

上海辰山植物园矿坑花园
The Quarry Garden in Shanghai Chenshan Botanic Garden

During the global environmental crisis of the 1960s, artists such as Robert Smithson revealed the sublime value of abandoned industrial places, and in 1969 Richard Haag's Gas Works Park in Seattle enshrined the beauty of such relics. In the 1990s Peter Latz went further by creating a post-industrial nature with his Duisburg-Nord Landscape Park in the Ruhrgebiet, Germany. Here, Latz brought out the capability of the place through the careful placement of new things with the old. The latest in this lineage is James Corner Field Operations' High Line in New York City.

Another kind of ruins appears more humble, somehow "dirty" and "ugly," yet bears a shift in deeper values. When visiting Rovira Hill in Barcelona, the honesty of the site deeply moves you. The notorious shantytown that once occupied the summit has nothing to do with heroism or political significance, but it was treasured for its "landscaping" process. Normally, things that have just lost their practical value are the least likely to be revered. It took 20 years for this site to be physically transformed, but how long have we spent to start realizing its capabilities? And what will be next?

急速城镇化进程中"美丽中国"的提出，标志着中国的整体建设转入了一个品质化的时期，对风景园林专业既是机遇，更是挑战。或许通过废墟再生现象，我们可以开启"潜质空间"的议题。所谓"潜质"，字面直解就是场地自身潜在的素质，可以被开发但尚未被开发；在设计师的预判下与整体目标挂钩，从而被激活、实现场地特质延续性的增值和升级。"capability(潜质)"取自"Capability Brown(万能布朗或潜质布朗)"，在18世纪英国的土地上，布朗唤现了一个自然风景园的空间价值维度，也收获了后巴洛克时代世界园林史上最为响a亮的绰号。当下看来，走向潜质空间最主要也最显见的路径，便是废墟再生。

1499年出版的奇书《Hypnerotomachia Poliphili》首次定格了废墟的美学价值，三百年后英国自然风景园和法国英中式花园中流行设计folly，废墟入园是如绘美学思潮向纵深化发展的结果。其实发现废墟潜质的意义很深远，因为隐含的推论是，只要是人类文明留下的遗迹就有被认可的可能。

废墟价值拓展的下一个对象就是近代工业文明。二十世纪六十年代世界环境危机时，罗伯特.史密森等艺术家

北京首钢矿坑遗址公园

Shougang Industrial Park in Beijing

The phenomenon of ruins is stated here for its easily interpreted contents. But the space of capabilities is more than just ruins, it is about layering dimensions of time and space. To designers, paying attention and moving toward the space with capability means a certain kind of design consciousness, and as landscape architecture's history attests, the people who first discover that potential will lead the transformation.

通过"微创"的设计干预，让大众发现荒野及工业废弃场地的价值。1971年理查德.黑格在西雅图瓦斯厂公园的设计中划时代地将废弃精炼厂的工业设施融入公园，俨然现代版的如绘folly。九十年代，彼得.拉茨走得更远，他洞见的是一个巨大、复杂又逻辑缜密的"工业自然"潜质系统，新事物的置入应与其历史脉络息息相关。标志着后工业景观成熟的杜伊斯堡工业园1994年首次开园，之后出现的便是空前成功的纽约高线公园。

另一种废墟看似丑陋，却隐含着深层价值观某种转向的可能性。笔者曾经登上巴塞罗那罗比拉山顶(Rovira Hill)，被其平实而又特殊的废墟气场深深撼动。这片声名狼藉的山顶棚户区与英雄主义或政治意义毫无关联，却在奥运会前城市景观化改造时被几乎原封不动地留存了下来，融入城市开放空间体系。刚刚失去现实价值的事物最不易让人心生敬畏，山顶棚户区从废弃到再利用仅仅走过20年，而人类迈出这一步又花了多长时间呢?废墟潜质利用的下一个大站会在哪里?

前文探讨的废墟现象可被视作潜质空间一个显见的例子，因为潜质空间绝不仅仅限于废墟，只是废墟空间更具备时空维度的层次感和可解读性。关注并走向潜质空间，对于设计师而言重要的是培养一种设计意识，之于风景园林，之于建筑，之于城市，也之于国家，都是相似相通的。历史发展证明，谁先发现潜质，谁将率先引领变革。

[illegible][illegible][illegible]亂

# 城市景观
# The Urban Landscape

# City Beautiful
# 美丽城市

**玛丽莲·泰勒** | Marilyn TAYLOR

Professor of Architecture and Urban Design, and former Dean, Stuart Weitzman School of Design, University of Pennsylvania. Over a 35-year career with Skidmore, Owings & Merrill, including as the firm's first woman chairman, Taylor led many of the firm's largest and most complex projects. Her research interests include the design of large-scale urban districts, transportation and infrastructure projects, and civic initiatives that act as catalysts of quality of life and economic vitality for cities and regions around the world.

宾夕法尼亚大学斯图尔特·威兹曼设计学院前系主任，建筑与城市设计方向教授。泰勒教授曾在SOM任职超过35年，并曾担任该公司的第一位女性总裁，领导完成了该公司最大最复杂的一系列设计项目。她的研究兴趣包括大尺度城市区片设计，交通与基础设施设计，以及能为世界各地提升生活质量经济活力的公民倡议。

When I first went to China more than three and a half decades ago it was not beautiful. Shanghai, where I landed, lay covered in a heavy cloud of industrial dust. The buildings on the Bund looked like ghosts. Windows were so dirty that no one could see in or out. Everything was gray. Since then, improvements have come: skies over Shanghai are not infrequently blue, glass curtain walls gleam, smart shops line curving shaded streets of gracious scale, fabrics are bold and colorful. This amazing Chinese city has transformed, and bloomed.

Yet, today Shanghai—along with the rest of the world—is in grave environmental crisis. In an immediate sense, this is not news. Sea rise, extreme storms and droughts, air pollution, and contaminated waters threaten the well-being of all things living. The causes are largely understood, but action is still slight in relation to the depth of the threat.

At the highest level, the leadership of China has established its commitment to becoming an "ecological civilization." President Xi Jinping has pronounced that "clear waters and green mountains are as good as mountains of gold and silver." This invocation has launched a proliferation of eco-friendly policies by Chinese state and local authorities. Waters and mountains evoke the concept of the large and continuous rural landscapes and the real and imagined urban gardens that have been pillars of value across millennia of Chinese art and culture.

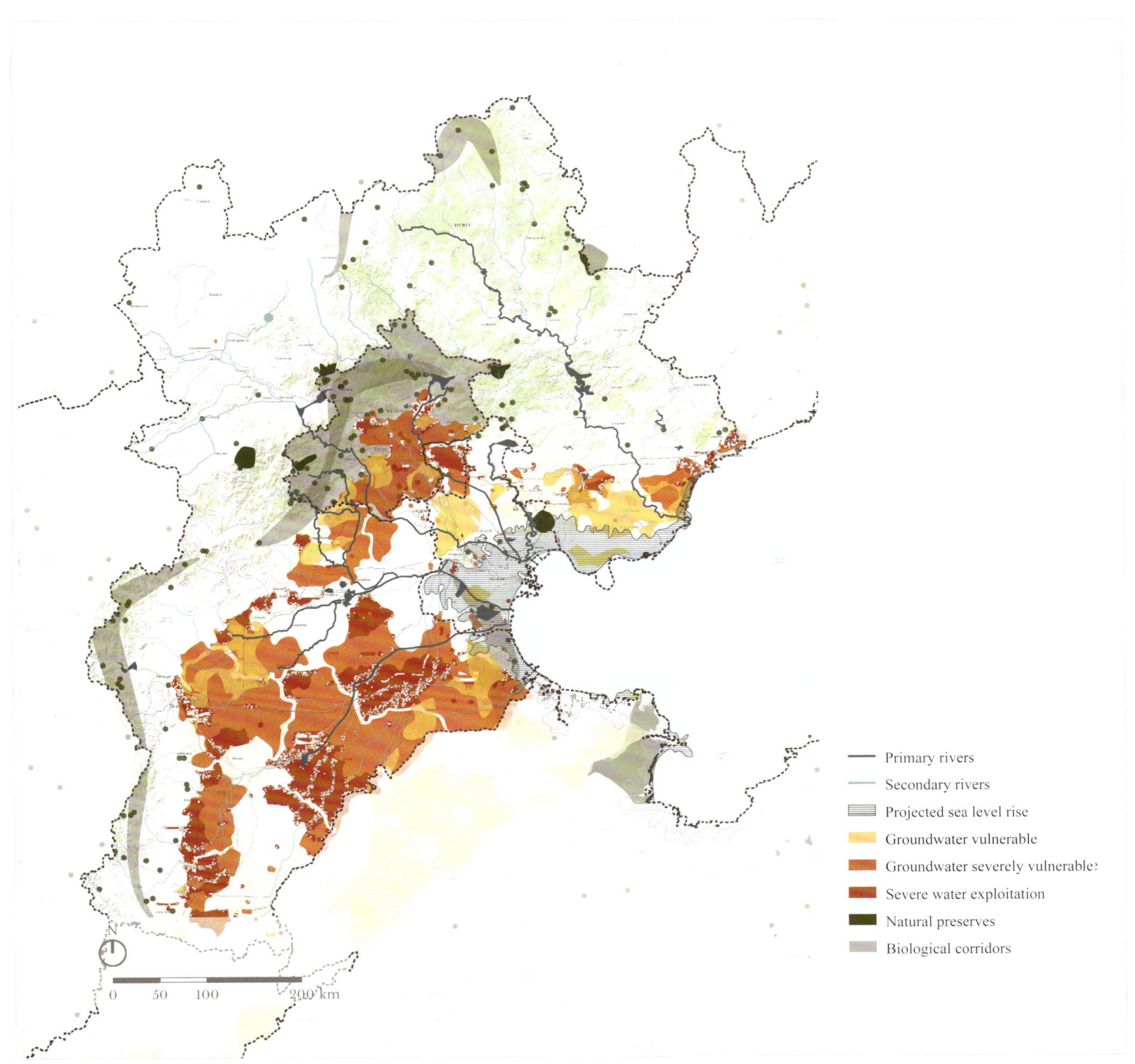


京津冀生态问题分析图

Ecological issues mapping of the Jing-Jin-Ji megaregion

区域快行捷运服务系统分析图
Proposed regional express service

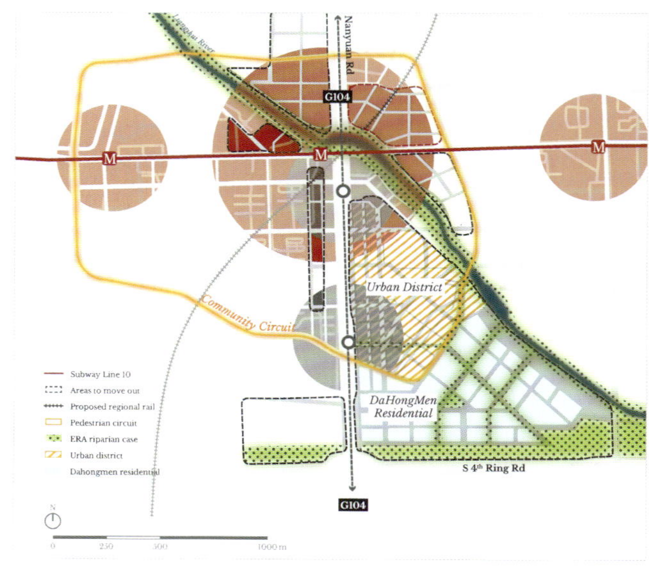


设计规划的中心、地区和公共生活示意图
Proposed centers, districts, and public life

当我三十五年前第一次造访中国时，那儿并不是美丽的。在上海登陆时，我看到那里仍然笼罩在一片浓重的工业尘埃之下——在外滩的建筑看起来像鬼屋一般。窗户很脏而不是透明的。一切都是灰色的。但自那以后，环境终于得以改善：上海的天空不只是偶尔的蓝色，玻璃幕墙闪闪发光，线条弯曲的现代商店隐匿在林荫道的阴影下，店铺里的面料缤纷多彩。这个令人惊叹的中国城市已经完全改变了，到处是欣欣向荣的景象。

然而，今天的上海以及世界其他地区，仍然处于严重的环境危机之中。从某种意义上说这也不算什么新闻。海平面上升、极端风暴和干旱、空气污染和水体污染，所有的这些都威胁着地球上的生物的福祉。虽然造成这些极端天气的原因大部分已经被我们所认识到，但是人们针对这些威胁采取的相关行动仍然是微不足道的。

在决策层的高度上，中国的领导者已经建立了致力于建设"生态文明"的目标。习近平主席宣称"绿水青山胜过金山银山"的这一呼吁已经逐渐在中国的国家与地方政府的生态友好政策中产生实质性的影响。江水和山

The foremost challenge of our century is to reverse environmental degradation and to restore the ecological function and beauty of the landscape. Can the ancestral roots of Chinese culture be brought into emerging technological prowess to reclaim that inheritance? Can the country's landscapes become the identifying characteristics for cities that are growing and changing? What is the role that design will play in advancing these critical initiatives?

A 2016 cross-disciplinary design studio offered at the Stuart Weitzman School of Design at the University of Pennsylvania posed three directions in which to move toward reclaiming the environment and its qualities, upon which viable human life depends. Students and professional advisors mapped the layers of environmental degradation across the Jing-Jin-Ji megaregion, a territory that encompasses 8% of China's population, 10.4% of its GDP, and 2.2% of its land area. The first initiative addressed the full geography of Jing-Jin-Ji by proposing a sweeping megaregional and provincial cooperative governmental initiative of restoration. The concept draws from two long-range and high-value 20th-century United States initiatives: (1) Theodore Roosevelt's creation of an expansive and protected National Park system, and (2) Franklin Roosevelt's Civilian Conservation Corps, which put thousands of men unemployed by the Great Recession of the 1930s to constructive work on environmental and infrastructural projects. Such a megaregion-wide initiative would accomplish essential restoration across the whole of Jing-Jin-Ji while also creating a new and high-value employment sector offering jobs in the restoration and care of parks, preserves, and agricultural lands. This would indeed be beautiful.

But, then, what about the cities themselves? As a second initiative, the studio team addressed the role of ecology within the city in a revised approach to the design and repair of neighborhoods and districts. The students put forward a design proposal for Beijing's Dahongmen District, between the third and fourth ring roads in the city's southeast. What became clear is that the redevelopment of an obsolete and underperforming neighborhood is inherently and necessarily a cultural, ecological, and social endeavor as well as an economic and political one.

Consistent with President Xi's directive to replace old, under-performing industries in Beijing with new and thriving economic generators, the Beijing district of Dahongmen was slated for extensive demolition and renewal, due to the aging out of wholesale markets for various goods including low-cost clothing. The studio's work demonstrates the potential of an alternative to sweeping demolition: reconfiguring the entire district and its market buildings to attract new clothing designers, studios, shops, and innovative manufacturers to the location. In this plan, some current businesses may decamp, but new ones will arrive to stimulate a synergy among local design and fabrication businesses and the creative economy. The physical reconfiguration offers places to live and work in a high-performance urban landscape that not only builds flood protection, but also provides for abundant open space and recreation that give the new Dahongmen district a healthier way of life. Within Dahongmen, the restoration of the

川，唤起了大型的、连续的乡村景观以及真实和想象的城市中的园林的概念，而这种园林的意向在数千年的中国艺术和文化中拥有举足轻重的地位。

本世纪最重要的挑战是——扭转环境恶化、恢复景观的生态功能和美感。能否在中国文化的根基之上，通过现在新兴的技术来重新发扬这种遗产的价值？这个国家的景观能否成为正在发展和变化的城市的重要特征？设计在推进这些关键举措方面将扮演什么角色？

宾夕法尼亚大学斯图尔特·威兹曼设计学院在2016年的跨学科设计工作室上提出了三个方案，旨在回归环境及其品质——而这正是人类生存所依赖的。学生和来自专业领域的导师绘制了京津冀大区的环境衰退图，该区域占中国人口的8%，占GDP的10.4%，占土地面积的2.2%。

第一个提议是通过提出全面的大规模和省级合作政府来进行重建的方案，试图解决京津冀的大部分地理问题。这个概念来自两个长期并高价值的20世纪美国倡议：(1)西奥多·罗斯福创建了一个广阔和受保护的国家公园系统；(2)富兰克林·罗斯福的平民保护团——使数千名失业者在20世纪30年代的经济大萧条中，能在环境和基础设施项目上开展建设性的工作。这样一个巨型城市范围的倡议将在整个京津冀实现显著的环境恢复效果，同时还能创造一个新的高价值就业部门，在恢复和养护公园、保护区和农业用地的同时提供就业机会。这一定会漂亮。

那么，对于城市本身呢？工作室团队的第二个提议是，通过修订的社区和地区设计和修复方法，发挥了城市生态学的作用。学生们提出了北京大红门区的设计方案，位于该市东南部的第三和第四环路之间。显而易见的是，对一个老旧的、表现不佳的社区的重建，本质上是一种文化、生态和社会的努力，也是一种经济和政治的努力。

与习近平主席指示的新的、蓬勃发展的产业经济取代北京旧的、表现不佳的产业一致的是，由于各种商品的批发市场（包括低成本服装在内的）逐渐老化，北京地区的大红门预计会进行大规模的拆迁和更新。该工作室的方案展示了替代大规模拆迁方案的潜力：重新配置整

能充分兼顾当地居民和游客需求的北京新城市化模式

A new urban plan for Dahongmen that accommodates the needs of both the local and transient populations

Liangshui River to improve water quality and floodwater management will be a strategic investment in resilience, offering urban trails, fields, and wetlands for relaxation, reflection, and recreation, for gathering and socializing places that bring the community together.

For their third initiative, the students singled out mobility. The vitality of Dahongmen can be better sustained by providing greater urban and regional connectivity. Most Chinese cities are relatively well served at both the local and national level by subways or buses, as well as by high-speed rail. However, rail commuting is less frequently provided for at the regional level. The system proposed by the Penn studio team would provide high-speed 30-minute to one-hour commuter rail trips among a network of highly concentrated employment centers across Beijing, as well as those in the nearby cities of Tianjin, Langfang, Zhuzhou, and Baoding. The result for Dahongmen and other highly connected Beijing districts can be a high-value mixed-use neighborhood, in which residents walk to work and school and where employees and customers arrive not only by the subway and bus, but also by a new regional commuter rail system.

Thus, a city district grows more viable and more beautiful from its economic and ecological roots.

个区域及其市场建筑，以吸引新的服装设计师、工作室、商店和创新产业进驻到该地点。在这个计划中，一些现有的企业可能会退出，但新的企业将会到来，以刺激当地设计和制造业务与创意经济之间的协同作用。物理空间的重新配置为高性能城市景观提供了生活和工作的场所，不仅可以建立防洪施舍，还提供丰富的开放空间和娱乐，为新的大红门区提供更健康的生活方式。在大红门，以改善水质和洪水管理为目标的凉水河的恢复计划将是一个战略性的提升城市恢复力投资，提供城市小径、田地和湿地去给市民放松、反思和娱乐、聚集和社交的场所，将社区群众聚集在一起。

第三种提议中，学生们特别地提出了流动性这一概念。通过提供更强大的城市和区域连通性，可以更好地维持大红门的活力。由于地铁、公共汽车以及高速铁路这一类的交通设施的建设，使得大多数中国城市在地方和国家层面的交通条件都得到了极大的改善。但是，在区域这一层级提供铁路通勤的频率较低。由此出发，宾大设计学院的工作室团队提出了一种交通系统，可以将在北京以及附近城市包括天津、廊坊、株洲和保定等地在内的高度集中的就业中心网络中提供高速的30分钟至1小时可达的通勤铁路网络。结果是，大红门和其他高度互联的北京地区可以成为一个高价值的综合用途社区，其中居民步行上班和上学，员工和顾客不仅能乘坐地铁和公共汽车，而且还能拥有一个新的区域通勤铁路系统。

因此，整个区域可以在其经济和生态的支撑下，变得更加富有生机，变得更加美好。

# Considering China's Future Public Realm
# 中国未来公共空间

**克里斯托夫·马辛考斯基 |**
Christopher MARCINKOSKI

Associate Professor of landscape architecture and urban design, University of Pennsylvania, and author of *The City That Never Was* (2016). Marcinkoski is a licensed architect and director of PORT, a public realm and urban design practice based in Philadelphia and Chicago. In 2015, he was awarded the Rome Prize in Landscape Architecture from the American Academy in Rome.

美国宾夕法尼亚大学景观建筑与区域规划系副教授，于2016年出版作品《未有之城》。马辛考斯基是美国注册建筑师与PORT事务所主创设计师，PORT事务所是一家专注于城市公共空间与城市设计实践的设计实践，分别在费城与芝加哥有分公司。在2015年，他获得了罗马美国学院景观建筑罗马奖。

Given my own academic and professional predilections, in the context of this volume exploring the notion of Beautiful China, I am compelled to briefly consider the potential implications of the initiative on the role of the public realm within contemporary Chinese urbanization. As has been described more comprehensively elsewhere in this collection, Beautiful China refers to President Xi Jinping's vision for an economic and societal "modernization…characterized by [the] harmonious coexistence between man and nature."[1] This vision, set out to be fully attained by 2035, is understood as a central component of China moving from a "moderately prosperous society" by 2020, to establishing itself as a "a great modern socialist country" by 2049 – the centenary of the founding of the People's Republic of China.[2] Notably for this essay, the benchmarks associated with the Beautiful China initiative and the 2035 and 2049 goals suggest both objective economic achievement and more subjective improvements in the quality of life of the country's population. Principally related to establishing models of urban and industrial production that are not environmentally degrading, the contours of the initiative emerged as early as 2012 during the 18th National Congress of the Chinese Communist Party as part of a basic framework for achieving what was described as an "ecological civilization."[3]

In contemporary Western discourse—particularly within landscape architectural practice and theory—discussions of beauty and ecology are oftentimes seen

as being incongruous. Considerations emerging from a principally scientific (environmental) perspective are, more often than not, seen as being of greater value than questions of aesthetics or beauty. These non-scientific concerns are pejoratively described as superficial and thin, in contrast to the depth and complexity—real importance—of ecological concerns.[4] Juxtapose this against President Xi's vision, which articulates a modernization that "provide[s] more quality ecological goods to meet people's ever-growing demands for a beautiful environment," a vision that essentially conflates the two concerns into one.[5]

Of course, in this context, it is important to consider the term "beautiful." In Xi's declarations, beautiful is employed as an overtly political rhetorical device. It originates, on the one hand, from ideals of environmental cleanliness and purity—as in the absence of air, soil, or water pollution—and, on the other hand, from a highly mediated perspective related to visual perception and identity – the aesthetic and aspirational values of China's "natural" landscapes. As such, I would suggest that the term beautiful within the Beautiful

由于我个人学术与实践的偏好，在探索"美丽中国"这一概念与其背景的过程中，我常思考这个概念在中国城市化背景下对公共空间的潜在影响。正如本书中其它文章更为详细的解读所阐述的一样，"美丽中国"这一概念是习近平主席对于中国经济与社会的"一种人与自然和谐共存的一种现代化"的展望[1]。这一理想被设定于在2035年完全建设完成，并将促使中国从2020年建设完成的"小康社会"，在新中国成立的100周年的2049年，转变为"一个伟大的社会主义国家"[2]。值得一提的是，在本文中，美丽中国政策与2035年和2049年的的发展目标的评价标准即包括了客观经济发展的指标，也包括了更加主观的对于人民生活质量提高的期待。这一政策以寻求一种不造成环境恶化的城市与产业发展模型为原则，作为国家发展的框架的一部分，最早于2012年的中国共产党第十八次全国代表大会被提出并被描述为中国的"生态文明"建设[3]。

在现代西方语境中，特别是在景观学科的理论与实践讨论中，美丽与生态常常被视为矛盾或不一致的两个概念，科学地对环境的考虑通常被认为比审美的思考更具价值。对比生态系统的复杂性与深度，关于美的思考作为非科学的考量因素常常被认为是肤浅单薄与无足轻重的[4]。与这种观念相对比，习近平主席将现代化解释为"为人民提供更多高质量的生态产品并满足人民对美好居住环境日益增长的需求"，这一观念却是将生态与美两方面的考量并置于同一高度的[5]。

理所当然，在这一背景下，对"美丽"这一概念的思考就变得尤为关键。在习近平主席的宣言中，美丽成为了一个明显的政治语汇。但在它原本的含义中，美丽，一方面指一种杜绝了空气，土壤与水污染的理想的纯净的居住环境，另一方面也暗喻了视觉的感知与文化认同感，同时具备在美学与精神层面中，中国"自然"景观的价值。因此，在我看来，美丽中国政策中，"美丽"这一概念，应当被理解为在精神层面上对理想自然环境，象征与文化认同和生活质量的追求，与在政治层面上，指导国家发展的政治语汇的一种结合。

除却其核心对于保护与减轻城市化与工业化带来的对城市周边与农村地区环境威胁的讨论，美丽中国的概念同样暗示了对于中国现代城市整体空间形态的考虑。习近平主席在2014年提出了有关中国城市景观环境发展的声明，在发言中，他公开指责了那些"奇奇怪怪的建筑"，并在之后2016年的国务院指导和中央全会中明确反对那些"超尺度和崇洋媚外"或与地域文化毫无关联的建筑[6]。从我们的角度来看，这两个政策，一个指向了自然环境的样貌，而另一个指向了城市环境的样貌，这似乎说明了习近平主席与其领导的中国共产党在尝试创造一种特定的中国21世纪城市物质空间的景观意象。但这一意象是怎样的呢？也许现在预测这一系列政策对于中国城市空间的改变的结果还为之过早，但我们却无疑可以尝试思考中国现代城市现存公共空间在这一政策背景下状态的变化。

我将从我对城市公共空间的定义来开始我的论述。在本文中，我所说的城市公共空间指的是城市中公众自发聚集的空间。公共空间，无论大小，通过居民或游客自发地徘徊与停留，并发生社交行为而产生，特别在中国的城市环境中，人们还会在这些空间中发生消费与交通穿越行为。这些空间包括了广场，步道，滨水空间，步行友好的街道，花园与绿道。大型的城市公园偶尔也被包括在这一定义中，特别是在他们与城市相接壤的边缘的空间。博览会与活动场所也是一个在中国各大都市中很常见的公共空间类型，但对于他们作为公共空间所能够发挥的真正

China initiative should be understood as a kind of politico-rhetorical mash-up of aspirational ideals of environment, image/identity, and quality of life.

Principally discussed in relation to the conservation and remediation of peri-urban and rural landscapes under threat from or already degraded by urbanization and industry, Beautiful China is also interesting to consider in terms of its implications for the collective spaces of contemporary Chinese cities. This is particularly true when it is considered in relation to another of President Xi's declarations regarding the identity of China's physical landscape, his 2014 public complaint about "weird architecture" and the subsequent 2016 directive from China's State Council, and the Communist Party's Central Committee that rejects public architecture that is "oversized, xenocentric" or unrelated to cultural tradition.[6] For our purposes, these two pronouncements, one ostensibly related to the appearance of the environment, and the other, the appearance of cities themselves, seem to suggest President Xi and the Communist Party are endeavoring to create a very particular physical identity for China's 21st-century urban landscape. But what exactly is this identity? While it is perhaps too soon to truly assess the consequences of these mandates on the form of Chinese cities, particularly the public realm of these cities, we can surely consider the extant status of these spaces within contemporary Chinese society.

Let me begin by first defining what I mean by referring to a city's public realm. Here, I am speaking about a city's spaces of spontaneous public collection. Those areas, large and small, where denizens and visitors recreate, socialize, linger, and, almost ubiquitously in the case of China, consume and transact. These spaces include plazas and promenades, waterfronts and walkable streets, gardens and greenways. Larger urban parks can sometimes fall under this definition, specifically their edges, where these spaces meet the surrounding urban fabric. Expo and event grounds are a common typology found across the major metropolises of China, but necessitate greater scrutiny in terms of their roles as true public space. Regardless of typological definition, these spaces can be publicly or privately maintained and

operated, and are generally open to anyone who abides by the expected social norms of the place.

It has been suggested many times that the public spaces of a city are the truest reflections of the priorities and predilections of its associated culture and society. As a riff on this idea, I would offer that I have had the opportunity to learn a great deal about public spaces in China, not only from visiting them, but also from how they are described by the numerous Chinese students who I have had the opportunity to teach over the last nine years. To illustrate these lessons, I'd like to share two experiences that have shaped how I have come to understand China's contemporary urban public realm.

The first is a near annual episode that occurs during the core urban design studio I coordinate at the University of Pennsylvania. The studio is predicated on using the public realm as a structuring device to guide urban (re)development. As part of this work, students are asked to both diagrammatically and three-dimensionally articulate a public realm framework as the basis of their individual proposals.

作用我们需要进行更加详细的审查。无论公共空间属于什么类型，他们既可以被政府也可以被私人开发商所运营或维护，但这些空间应该依据社会准则所期待的一样对所有停留徘徊的人们开放。

公共空间常常被认为是一个城市与其主流文化和社会形态的真实反映。通过多次对中国的访问与过去九年来大量的中国学生口中的描述，我有机会造访和学习了许多中国的公共空间的案例，并重复多次验证了这一理论。下文我将通过我的两个经历来阐述我今天对于中国现代城市公共空间的认知是如何形成的。

第一个经历是来自于我在宾夕法尼亚大学指导的一年一度的核心设计课程——城市设计课程。这个课程希望引导学生学习如何利用公共空间作为指导城市（再）发展的框架与工具。作为这个课程的一部分，学生们被要求用二维图示与三维模型的方法设计一个公共空间框架作为他们进一步城市设计方案的基础。不变的是，年复一年，在中国学生所设计的方案中，总有相当一部分人会提出下述两种设计策略中的其中一种，有时甚至是两种策略同时出现。第一种是被零售商业活动所主导的公共空间。第

Invariably, year in and year out, a significant number of projects developed by Chinese students propose one of two things—though often both simultaneously. The first is a public realm principally dominated by retail activities. The second is a public realm that is vertically stacked, multi-layered, and disengaged—whole or in part—from the adjacent street network.

Given that the project sites for these studios are typically located in North America, these propositions are inevitably met with declarations of concern by incredulous studio critics – retail-driven public space is not truly public as it requires an expenditure of capital in order to participate, they say; or, public space that cannot be accessed directly from the street will inevitably fail due to a limited audience, they demand. But these declarations are, of course, really only true in a Western context. What my Chinese students are proposing, unsurprisingly, is precisely what they have experienced first-hand as public realm in the two-plus decades of their lifetimes – expansive, multi-layered, consumption-driven urban spaces of spectacle.

Interestingly, the second anecdote I offer about this same demographic seems to sit in direct contrast to the first. As part of a studio I conducted in 2018, I had the opportunity to take 12 students to visit a collection of cities in the Pearl River Delta. Eight of these students were Chinese nationals, but only two had ever been to this region of the country. As we visited Hong Kong, Guangzhou, and Shenzhen, a pattern quickly emerged. While I would propose visiting recently completed public spaces, or notable pieces of contemporary architecture, the students' repeated preference was to search out so-called urban villages and more intimate and hidden spaces of these urban landscapes, generally resisting what might be considered the grand or signature public spaces of each city.

While this might be the result of a generational interest in the novel or unique—Instagram culture—I believe this preference is indicative of something larger. Essentially, the spaces that my students so often refer to in their own design projects—whether intentionally or not—were being treated as far less interesting than what one might call the quotidian spaces of the Pearl River

二种是垂直堆叠的多层公共空间，并且这种立体公共空间将局部或整体的脱离于相邻的街道网络系统。

由于课程的场地往往位于北美地区，这些设计主张常常会不可避免地被课程汇报时的评审们所质疑，一是他们认为被商业活动主导的空间由于其需要一定的消费才能参与或使用的性质使得它并不能被称作真正的公共空间，二是他们坚信不能从城市街道上直接联通到达的公共空间会由于缺少使用者而注定失败。然而，这些主张当然只能在西方城市语境下成立。我的中国学生们提出的策略，不出所料的，是他们二十多年来日常在中国所亲身经历与认知的公共空间，一种昂贵的，立体的，消费主导的城市空间奇观。

有趣的是，第二个我要讲述的有关于中国学生的有趣经历却似乎与第一个经历截然相反。作为2018年我指导的一个设计课程的一部分，我有机会带领了12个学生去珠三角地区参观了一系列城市。这些学生中的其中八个是中国公民，但只有两个曾经去过中国的珠三角地区。当我们在参观香港，广州和深圳时，学生们的偏好很快地显现出来。当我建议参观一些最新建设完成的公共空间项目或是著名的现代建筑时，学生们多次提出他们更想要去探索类似于城中村一类的更加隐秘的城市景观，同时对造访每个城市中被认为是宏伟的标志性城市景观表现出抗拒。

也许这是由于社交媒体所造成的这一代人对于新奇和独特事物的偏好，但我相信学生们对隐秘与独特城市公共空间的兴趣暗示着更深远的意义。从本质上来说，学生们通常在他们的设计方案中参考的空间，不管是否是有意识的，都被认为比珠三角大都市中的一个日常场所无趣的多。那些他们经常在城市设计中多次提到的城市空间被忽视，而那些不卫生的，粗糙的，并且非常陈旧的空间却更能激起他们的兴趣。虽然此时我们应该警惕通过这两个例子中如此小的样本中得出任何结论，但我能感觉到，相对于我们在讨论中国城市现代公共空间常想到的那些宏伟的，超尺度的，纪念性的空间，这一代人对于老旧的，小尺度的隐藏空间偏好对中国公共空间的未来发展的意义是非比寻常的。

我将我们所见证的中国城市化特征总结为四个关键词：尺度，速度，奇观性与超级性。从这方面来说，我前文所提到的大部分中国学生都成长于这样一个无情的，消费主导的城市化过程中，这样的城市化往往抹去场地原有的文脉，忽略场地的地形，气候，生物与土壤环境，只追求一种缺乏场所感的，理想化的现代化。然而这种理想化的现代城市图景的追求所存在于的纯粹景观空间，却成为了中国当权者对于美丽的新的追求与对怪异的反对的新主张的实施目标。也就是说，当权者的真正兴趣或真正的讨论，在政治的舞台上，更多的是对于中国无论是人文或是自然的物理空间的全方位控制。

无论在任何一个文化背景下，对于公共空间的讨论，明显是离不开对于政治与社会问题的思考的，在中国的文化与社会背景下，政治与社会特征更是在讨论中表现的尤为突出。我承认，作为一个西方设计师，我所处的视角不足以让我完全的参与到全面的讨论之中，我也不怀疑本书是一个理想的讨论本话题的场所。但是，当我们思考中国的公共空间时，除却那四个关键词，另一个非常重要的方面，是在西方城市公共空间构建中最为核心的文化品质的明显缺失，在这个背景下，以西方传统广场的游散性为例[7]，虽然商业活动也存在于这一古老的公共空间类型中，但它并不是主导的，且其更有活力与效率的值得推敲的品质显然不存在于中国现代的城市公共空间之中。

在这一现实之下，那我们应该怎样在美丽中国的政策背景下，思考中国的公共空间呢?当上一辈的中国景观设计师正将他们在西方所接受的麦克哈格式的对于环境与保护的观念带回中国时，我假定当代中国设计师在西方所接受的训练和教育将会是非常不同的。他们大部分成长于新中国的大都市而非农村地区，我不认为他们对于城市的兴趣会更多的存在于生活质量与宜居空间上。如果要我猜测当这一代景观设计师成为学术与实践上的领军人物之时，他们的关注点会在何处，我认为对于环境的担忧固然会存在，但中国城市公共空间的根本性转变将是他们的奋斗目标。

正如西方的景观设计师在20世纪末与21世纪初不断尝试去弥补现代化(包括工业，交通运输与提炼等产业)所带来的意料之外的副作用时，我认为这一代的中国设计师也将为弥补与缓解过去30年狂妄的实用主义城市规划所驱动的中国城市化所带来的副作用而耗费很多努力。这些努力是我认为将会真正引领中国走向美丽中国的途径，是为居民不断创造高质量生活的努力，而不仅仅是创造一副图景。

Delta metropolises we visited. The spaces my students have repeatedly referenced as design propositions being ignored in favor of the unsanitized, gritty, and—notably—timeworn alternatives. Now, obviously one needs to be extremely cautious in drawing conclusions from the small sample sizes of these two examples, but my sense is that there is something of significance to this seeming generational preference for the old, small, and hidden over the vast, scale-less, and monumental we so often think of when discussing the contemporary public realm of China's cities.

The urbanization we have witnessed in China over the last 30 years can be described by what I would characterize as the four S's – Scale, Speed, Spectacle, and Superlatives. As such, the majority of the students to which I am referring have grown up in the context of a relentless, consumption-based urbanization that has often erased cultural texture and ignored physiographic, climatic, biotic, and edaphic conditions in favor of an idealized, albeit increasingly placeless, modernization. It is the pursuit of this idealized image of the contemporary city and in turn, the pure landscape in which it sits, that seems to be at the core of the drive by those in power in China for beauty and against the weird. That is, the interest seems to be as much about real conservation—environmental or architectural—as it is political stagecraft, using these pronouncements to project a sense of control over physical territory near and far, be it anthropogenic or naturogenic.

There are obviously very large social and political questions that relate to the discussion of public realm in any context, but particularly so in a milieu like China. And I would acknowledge that perhaps my position as a Western designer likely does not qualify me to fully engage these aspects. Nor do I suspect that that this is the ideal venue for such a discussion. However, when one begins to think of China's urban public realm, the aspect that is perhaps most striking—beyond the four S's—is the conspicuous absence of the very qualities that we hold up in the West as being central to the cultural value of any city's public realm – what I will refer to in this context as the discursive qualities of the agora.[7] While commerce is certainly present—if not dominant—in these spaces, the other more productively abrasive attributes of this ancient typology clearly are not.

Given this reality, how then should we think about the future of China's urban public realm in the context of Beautiful China? While an older generation of Chinese landscape architects likely took McHargian lessons of environment and conservation back with them from their Western educations, I would posit that the legacy of the current generation of Chinese designers being educated and trained in the West will be very different. Having principally grown up not in rural areas but in the urban metropolises of new China, I suspect their interests relate more to quality of life and habitable spaces of the city. Environmental concerns certainly remain, but if I were to wager a guess at what this generation's principal professional and academic endeavors will be as they move into positions of leadership, I would suggest it will be the fundamental transformation of the collective spaces of China's cities.

Like the Western landscape architects and designers who have spent the better part of the late 20th and early 21st centuries attempting to undo the unintended effects of modernization—be they industry, transportation, or extraction-related—I suspect that this generation of Chinese designers will exert a great deal of effort on undoing and mitigating the relentless effects of the megalomaniacal functionalist urban planning that has driven Chinese urbanization over the last 30 years. It is this work that I suspect will lead to truly achieving a Beautiful China. One based in producing a truly high quality of life for a population, not just the image of one.

1. Nagai O., "China's Xi Outlines Vision of Great Modern Socialist Country," *Nikkei Asian Review* (October 18, 2017), https://asia.nikkei.com/Economy/China-s-Xi-outlines-vision-of-great-modern-socialist-country.
2. Ibid.
3. Bosu R.S., "China Redoubles Efforts Toward 'Beautiful China' by 2035," *China Plus* (May 22, 2018), http://chinaplus.cri.cn/opinion/opedblog/23/20180522/134276.html.
4. Rolston H., "From Beauty to Duty: Aesthetics of Nature and Environmental Ethics," in Berleant A. (ed.), *Environment and the Arts: Perspectives on environmental aesthetics* (Hampshire, UK: Aldershot, 2002) 127–31.
5. "CPC Incorporates 'Beautiful China' into Two-Stage Development Plan," *China Daily* (October 18, 2017), http://www.chinadaily.com.cn/china/2017-10/18/content_33404172.htm.
6. Li C., "China Moves to Halt Weird Architecture," *New York Times* (February 22, 2016), https://www.nytimes.com/2016/02/23/world/asia/china-weird-architecture.html.
7. Whyte W., *City: Rediscovering the Center* (Philadelphia: University of Pennsylvania Press, 2009).

# Park City
# 公园城市

**成玉宁 | CHENG Yuning**

Dean, Department of Landscape Architecture, Southeast University, Nanjing. Cheng has been awarded the title of Design Master by the government of Jiangsu Province. He is also a council member of the Chinese Society of Landscape Architecture and deputy director of its education committee. Cheng has authored many national and provincial scientific research projects, seven books, and more than 80 papers, and has won over 30 national and provincial awards.

东南大学建筑学院景观学系主任，江苏省设计大师，兼任中国风景园林学会理事、中国风景园林学会教育专委会副主任。近年来，主持多项国家及省部级科研项目，完成风景园林规划设计、风景园林设计等工程实践百余项，发表学术论文80余篇，先后获国家及省部级设计奖近30余次。

The Park City concept proposed by Chinese President Xi Jinping symbolizes the promising vision of the sustainable development of urban living environments in China. It advocates scientific urban planning to realize the goal of building high-quality human settlements. Park City aims to achieve the coordinated development of urban ecology and urban form through scientific planning strategies, design concepts, and design methods.

During the past four decades of reform, China's urban and rural areas have experienced unprecedented development, with an emphasis on the construction of human settlements. This development has gone through three stages: Garden City, Ecological Garden City, and Park City. The urban design and planning approaches of the three stages are different. Traditionally, the construction of cities is focused on pragmatic matters such as water supply and drainage, energy supply, transport and communication needs, and land leveling. After the city has been built we insert artificial green spaces, or parks, into the city – this is the approach of Garden City and Ecological Garden City. Park City advocates a different strategy: it seeks to protect the natural environment and form, letting nature do its own work with moderate human intervention and adding urban functions to create a city within a park.

The planning and construction of Park City is based on a scientific evaluation of the ecological sensitivity of the land and subsequent judgment about suitability of urban land use, taking into account local conditions. Land-use suitability theory is well developed in China (see, for example, *The Rites of Zhou*), and Park City inherits the idea that the land should be used for the purpose most suited to it—whether that be forestry, agriculture, industry, or urban habitation—thus providing an empirical and scientific basis for urban planning to large-scale territorial planning. The performance evaluation index of Park City is also empirical. It does not simply assess the quantitative data of discrete elements or rely upon the traditional flat index system used in urban planning. Instead, it considers complex factors of system operation efficiency integrating various indexes of urban spatial form, ecological environment, and social economy.

Every city is to some degree the result of the integration of the natural ecological environment and the artificial environment. The urban ecosystem is mainly about the interdependence of

中国国家领导人习近平总书记提出的公园城市，标志着我国城乡人居环境可持续发展的美好愿景。同时倡导以科学的城市规划，来实现建设高品质人居环境的目标。公园城市具有全新的内涵，其内涵是经由科学的规划设计理念与方法，来实现城市生态与形态的协同发展。

改革开放四十年间，中国城乡获得了前所未有的大发展，并且十分重视人居环境建设。先后经历了园林城市、生态园林城市与公园城市三大阶段。三大阶段的路径与策略不尽相同。其中园林城市到生态园林城市，突出表现为重视绿地的增量；由于城市系统具有复杂性与多功能复合性的特征，公园城市地提出要求城市空间建构应达到多功能与多目标彼此协调同，实现城市的生态本底与人工营造的生态环境对城市功能区块有效补充和支撑，这是城市发展的新阶段。公园城市倡导人、城、境、业高度和谐的新城市形态。传统城市建设往往是“三通一平，四通一平，五通一平，甚至七通一平”，最终把自然环境“格式化”，城市建设好后再去植入绿地，所谓的人化自然，与之相应“园在城中”。公园城市倡导不同的策略，保护自然格局、最大限度地让自然做工，通过适度的人为干预优化自然环境，在此基础上融入城市功能，

事半功倍，“城在园中”。其中“园”首先是自然本底，其次是人为的补充与协调，将自然环境作为美好家园的最基本的组成部分。

公园城市规划建设基于对环境的认知，其核心在于科学评价与判断城市用地生态敏感性与适宜性。其中用地生态敏感性是认知的前提，在此基础上探讨土地利用的适宜性，切实做到因地制宜。也就是宜林则林、宜农则农、宜居则居、宜商则商。中国农耕文明很发达，《周礼》中已有大量的文字描述“地宜”的理念，也称“土宜说”。公园城市传承了地尽其宜的理念，引领城市规划走向科学化。大尺度的国土规划、空间规划正是基于土地的生态敏感性探讨土地利用适宜性，这也是对于以传统功能导向为主的城市规划模式的超越。

任何一座城市都是结合用地的原生态规划发展而来的，是自然生态环境与人工环境的融合。就城市生态系统而言，主要体现在与地形地貌、水资源的耦合以及顺应自然的演替规律。城市环境现有的地形地貌特征是人工营建与自然长期作用的结果，构成了城市自然与文化景观。城市的发展需要巧妙结合自然，充分利用原有

geographic and geomorphic conditions, such as topography, water resources, and processes of vegetation succession. The existing geographic and geomorphic features of an urban environment are the result of long-term effects of artificial construction and nature, which constitute the natural and cultural landscape of a city. Urban development needs to utilize nature wisely; only by protecting and restoring the original topography, the hydrological system, and plant communities can we construct the foundation of an ecological urban environment. Through the simulation of self-renewing natural plant communities with stable structures, strong ecological functions, and low maintenance we can achieve sustainability in cities.

Taking water as another example, the natural hydrological process and water system are closely related to precipitation and topography. The relationship between mountains and rivers is formed by the long-term action of natural elements. Blind urban expansion changes the natural hydrological system and is the fundamental cause of urban flood and drought. Urban development must reconcile with the water environment, managing surface and groundwater effectively by promoting the natural infiltration, accumulation, purification, utilization, and discharge of rainwater.

City life depends on the sustainable development of the ecological environment. The construction of a Park City is based on the premise of protecting and optimizing the urban ecological environment, so that the urban environment has the ecological effect of imitating nature, thus ensuring the benign cycle of the urban ecological system. After a healthy ecological environment is realized, focus can turn to urban land use organization and optimized urban spatial form to achieve the appropriate coupling of urban ecology and urban form.

地形地貌。因此保护和恢复场地原有地形地貌、水文系统与植物群落，建构城市环境生态的本底。在此基础上通过模拟自然植物群落、恢复地带性植被等方式是实现城市环境可持续性的有效途径。因此城市中需要建构起结构稳定、生态功能强、养护成本低、具有良好自我更新能力的植物群落。

再以水为例，自然界中的水文过程、水系与降水及地形关系密切，山水关系是自然要素长期作用而形成的，盲目的城市扩张会改变天然的水文系统及其过程，是城市水旱灾害的根本原因。城市发展必须妥善处理水环境，要有效利用地表水和地下水。同时海绵化城市下垫面，促进对雨水的自然渗透、积存、净化、利用和排放。

城市生活有赖于生态环境的持续发展。建设公园城市首先以保护、优化城市生态环境为前提，使城市环境具有拟自然的生态效应，从而确保城市生态系统的良性循环。在此基础上探讨城市用地布局、优化城市空间形态，寻求城市生态与形态的耦合，是公园城市的基本特征。

# The Garden Laboratory
# 地被生境实验室

**刘晖 | LIU Hui**

Professor and Discipline Leader of Landscape Architecture, College of Architecture, Xi'an University of Architecture and Technology. Liu's research is focused on the theory and history of Chinese landscape culture, the theory and method of landscape planning and design in arid and semi-arid areas, and the evolution of urban form of Xi'an since 1949. Liu has presided over three National Natural Science Foundation research projects and is author or co-author of over 40 papers and seven books.

教授，博士，博士生导师，西安建筑科技大学建筑学院，风景园林学科带头人。从事风景园林专业教育，三个学术研究方向：中国地景文化理论与历史，干旱半干旱地区景观规划设计理论与方法，西安近现代城市形态演进。主持"西北城市绿地生境多样性营造多解模式设计方法研究"等3项国家自然科学基金课题，合作编著《中国地景文化史纲图说》《现代世界中的古老城市：西安——城市形态的演变1949-2000》等著作7部，发表论文40余篇。

The ecological and social quality of urban green space is a key aspect of Beautiful China and an important topic in relation to the quality of life in contemporary China. It is also a practical field of research where prototypes for the most effective form of greenery need to be developed in relation to the different regional ecologies of China. The ecological matrix in northwest China, for example, is dominated by groundcover plant communities and is suitable for small-scale site construction in urban green space planning. My research focuses on developing planting prototypes suited to urban environments in this region.

Since 2003, I have been conducting this research in a working garden that functions as an open laboratory within the campus of Xi'an University of Architecture and Technology. Through years of observation and experiments with 1 meter x 1 meter plots we have been able to measure the ecological and aesthetic value of different groundcover plant communities and their feasibility for use in construction projects. Based on this research, I developed two small-scale community groundcover planting models, one with more human intervention and one with a composition of spontaneous local groundcover plants. Although, the spontaneous groundcover model required less human intervention, after three years' observation, we found that, with more human intervention the moisture can be held in the soil better, which is important for developing a successful groundcover in the semi-arid area of China. Throughout the process of its construction and continuous optimization, the

地被植物季向模型
Groundcover plant community in different seasons

garden laboratory has extensively influenced teachers and students and attracted the attention and interest of the surrounding residents. Teachers and students not only design, construct, and maintain the garden, but also carry out the measurement and drawing of the external space of the site, observe the evolution of plant communities, and carry out planting design and maintenance.

During festival times, the garden is elaborately decorated and becomes the public focus of the university, and a part of community life. At the same time, the garden also enhances the awareness of the surrounding residents about plant ecology. Eighty-five percent of the residents who entered the garden were attracted by the plants in the garden, and seventy-seven percent found the garden to be an educational experience. In addition, visitors also express their desires for gardens, and some ask about the professions of garden design and landscape architecture.

Drawing on the results of the research we can summarize the following key points in regard to the ecological design of urban projects. The first step is to determine the appropriate habitat types and relate them to the site function. The second step is to design the types and forms of groundcover plant community composition based on the design of landscape elements and their spatial layout, and to create the spatial layout according to both ecological and aesthetic values. The third step is to design the implementation of the planting according to the needs of the project. Finally, in order to promote the succession and relative stability of the groundcover plant

城市的绿地规划建设的生态与社会品质是“美丽中国”在有关健康优美人居环境营建的重要内容，是服务生态园林城市、城市双修、海绵城市、公园城市等国家战略的实践领域。其中，中国西北地区多以地被植物群落为生态基质原型，在城市绿地规划中小尺度场地得建设中具有独特性和适宜性。在城市建成环境中，绿地有多种类型，其中嵌在城市建成环境中的破碎化小型绿地和地被植物群落具有城市生态系统建设的价值。我的研究主要关注于西北地区城市建成环境中，地被植物群落种植原型的设计。

自2003年16年以来，我于西安建筑科技大学的校园内建设了两个生境营造的实验基地。通过近3年对1m x 1m的样方的实验及观测研究，我们发现了不同地被植物群落组构的生态价值和美感度的可行性及其设计模式。根据研究，我们选择了两种不同适宜中国建设的植物群落种植模式，即“人工地被植物群落组构”和“自生地被植物群落组构”。其中人工地被植物需要更多的人工干预，通过人工覆盖物可以有效保持土壤水分，从而在西北半干湿地区获得更丰富的植物的景观效果，并在凋零期能够维持景观的可持续性。虽然，自生地被植物群落更具有自然荒野的特点，但通过人工干预措施，也能够更容易的形成地被覆盖，并增加植物群落的美感度。

在其建设过程和不断的变化中，基地广泛影响了专业师生和周边居民的关注和兴趣。师生们不仅设计、建设和维护花园，并开展场地测绘，观察植物群落演变，制作自然笔记，为专业师生提供了教学场所。节日期间，精心装点的花园又成为举校瞩目的活动场所，花园已成为

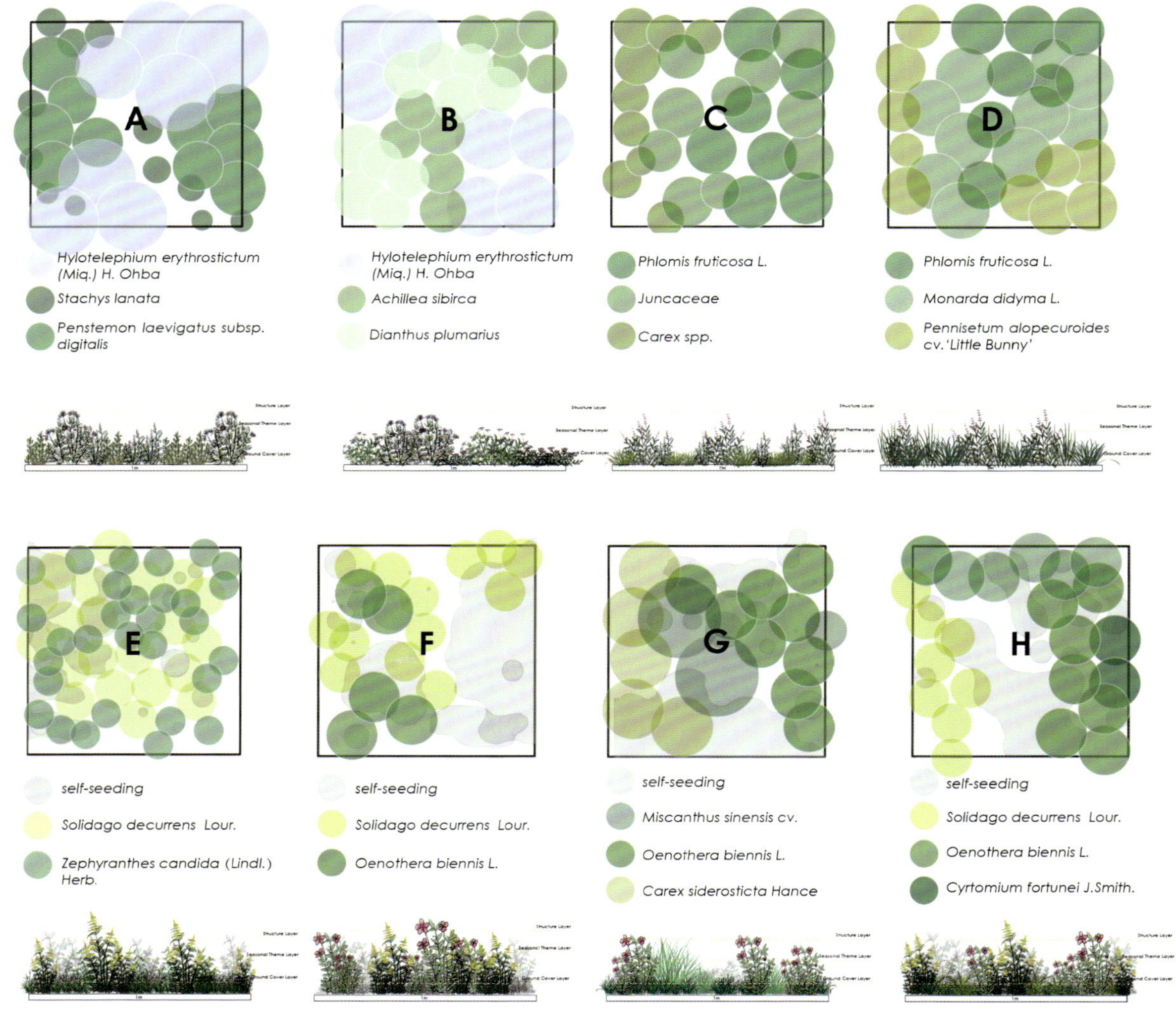


地被植物组成模型
Groundcover plant community composition model

community, there must be an ongoing maintenance and management plan to ensure plant succession.

Despite progress there are still many challenges in applying ecological knowledge to the design and construction of the built environment in China. Advances in Chinese landscape architecture are complicated by the difficulty of cross-disciplinary cooperation, as well as by the ways in which landscape is generally perceived in popular culture in China. In the implementation of the Beautiful China strategy we need to be mindful of connotations of beauty if we are to realize the ecological and social benefits it intends. The construction of Beautiful China is not only dependent on carrying forward Chinese traditional culture, but also lies in realizing the scientific value of the beautiful, and using landscape architecture to create social, ecological, and educational places. Beautiful China in landscape architecture is about ensuring that all people have access to beauty.

社区生活的一部分。同时，花园也提高了周围居民对植物生态知识的公众认知度。进入花园的居民中有85%是被植物吸引，有77%的人认为在进入花园之后是可以学习到植物和生态学的知识。另外，他们也会主动表达自己对花园的诉求，并询问花园设计与管理者的职业，从多角度理解风景园林学科专业。

我们在建成环境生境营造实验实践过程，提出生境营造基本程序及内容。第一步，结合场地分析与功能分区，评估分析“场地生境类型”，进行“场地生境分区”；第二步结合景观要素设计及其空间布局，进行“地被植物群落组构”类型及形态设计，并根据生态和美学绩效需求进行空间布局；第三步结合工程实施需求，进行“地被植物群落建植”实施方案设计；最后是维护管理，为了促进地被植物群落演替达到相对稳态，展开年度季节性的“连续性设计”和“演替维护”。

建成环境生态系统建设的研究存在于多个学科和实践领域中，设计营建类的学科领域对于生态学知识的实践应用具有很多挑战。中国风景园林学科面对跨专业合作、中西文化语境、社会公众景观偏好的文化背景等方面的挑战，其实际应用的需求也是巨大的，提出适宜的设计语言显得尤为重要。因此，美丽中国需要不断地认知“美丽”的内涵，实现生态、社会效益是建立美丽中国的基本需求，建设美丽中国不仅有赖于发扬中国传统文化，还应践行科学价值的“美丽”，以及日常生活环境中建设社会公众对“美丽”的科学教育场所，美丽中国之于风景园林，是每一个人、每一个群体对于美丽的理解、追求和享用。

社會景觀

# 社会景观
# The Social Landscape

MEOW

BROOKLYN

# Participatory Construction of Public Urban Landscapes
## 中国的社区参与式景观营造探索

**刘悦来** | LIU Yuelai

Senior Lecturer, Tongji University, and Principal of Shanghai Clover Nature School. Liu holds a PhD in Planning and Urban Design with his primary areas of research being community gardens and sustainable urban landscape planning and design. In recent years, he has actively promoted the participatory design and construction of public space in cities, with his team assisting communities to construct local gardens in more than 60 sites in Shanghai.

同济大学景观学系学者，上海四叶草堂青少年自然体验中心理事长，研究方向为可持续景观规划。近年来以自然教育为线索，以社区花园为空间更新实验基地，积极推动参与式设计营建，进行社区自组织景观的推广与探索，促进多元共治机制下的基层社区自治。目前团队已经在上海营造了六十余处社区花园。

**许俊丽** | XU Junli

Post-doctoral researcher, Shanghai Clover Nature School. Xu's research focuses on urban ecology ecosystem health, the sustainable development of community gardens, and natural education.

上海四叶草堂青少年自然体验服务中心研究专员，研究方向为城市生态学，生态系统健康，社区花园可持续发展和自然教育。

As one kind of green space, community gardens play a positive role in addressing many issues in the development of high-density cities, including constraints on limited available resources and environment, sustainable development, community building, and nature education. As such, community gardens are a humble but important means of connecting the national policy of Beautiful China to local urban communities. Over four years of practice, our team has created more than 60 community gardens in Shanghai. This essay discusses two typical cases, Baicao Garden, a community-run garden supported by the government, and the Knowledge and Innovation Community Garden, a public neighborhood garden supported by private enterprise. Our research was designed to explore different strategies for creating community gardens in current high-density downtown areas in China.

The Baicao Garden project is located in the Third Neighborhood of Anshan Fourth Village, Yangpu District, Shanghai, and serves the community of a dense residential area established in the 1970s. The Tongji University and Siping Sub-district chose the Baicao Garden as a demonstration site for community empowerment and introduced a non-governmental organization, the Clover Nature School, to take part in community empowerment activities in 2016.

The government design department and the residents' committee joined the Baicao Garden project early on and launched an internal consultation mechanism. They held meetings at every level from the sub-district office to the local residents (including children), breaking down barriers of communication among residents and between residents and decision-makers. They also went on neighborhood visits and listened to the opinions of large numbers of residents, and subsequently adjusted the plan for the garden. The local Fangling Flower Club was also involved in the design process, encouraging even more children and adults to become involved. The outcome was a space designed to meet the needs of residents for leisure activities, parent–child interaction, and nature education.

Following discussions, the design team selected a central green space with an area of 200 square meters for construction of Baicao Garden. Because the high-density environment in which the garden is located already takes a psychological toll on the people that live there, it was decided that the landscaping improvements should start

社区花园作为一种城市绿地形式，对于高密度城市发展过程中需要解决的众多问题，包括可持续发展、社区营造、自然教育等议题有着积极的作用。2014年起作者团队在上海协助不同类型的社区建设了有60余处社区花园，基于五年的时间，本文主要选择由政府支持的"住区自治型"——百草园和企业支持的"公共街区型"——创智农园作为案例，探讨当下中国高密度中心城区城市空间社区花园营造策略。

百草园，位于杨浦区四平路街道鞍山四村第三小区内，是建于20世纪60年代的密集型居住区。2016年，以街道牵头出资，由同济大学景观学系设计，社会公益组织四叶草堂提供运营管理支持，居民共建共享完成。

方案设计过程中，设计团队与居委会共建内部议事平台，打通居民之间、居民与决策者之间的沟通屏障，不断深入社区现场进行访谈，征询大量居民意见，确定最终方案。在反复沟通中，设计团队逐渐理解景观回归日常生活的基础是不增加居民的生活压力，留给居民更多的自主空间和未来更多的变化空间。社区花园改造伴随着众多社会问题，需要更深入地与居民沟通。

设计团队选择占地200平方中心绿地作为突破点营造百草园。百草园是取百家之花，造千人之园地之意。百草园营造过程中注重居民参与，充分发挥社区已有芳邻花友会的作用，带动了更多小朋友和成年人共同参与。基本没有施工经验的居民花了一个月的时间完成了百草园的建设。通过多次组织活动，百草园形成了小小志愿者团队参与百草园日常维护，加深了孩子们对社区及社会的责任，已成为社区营造和花园管理的活跃力量。此外，百草园和打虎山路小学合作将百草园作为学校的自然教育基地，并与鞍山363弄的芳草园实现了活动资源共享，拉近了邻里互动关系。

社区花园建设的初衷是建立相互学习的机制，使花园变成Learning Garden，真正使得社区居民从小开始，由单纯的消费者逐渐变成积极的参与者、生产者。自治型社区花园的成熟标准是有没有形成有自治能力的群众社团组织，社团数量越多、活动内容越丰富、管理制度越规范，包容性就越大，居民的参与性就越高。该案例作为上海老旧小区空间改善的探索，为人口高密度、居民老龄化和景观提升难度高等同类型社区提供了新的解决思路和管理模式。

创智农园（以下简称农园）是位于上海市杨浦区五角场街道创智天地园区一处废弃地上的社区花园[1]。其定位为“社区互动空间”，是上海市首个位于开放街区中的社区花园[2]。它的互动活力得益于功能的多样性，服务于交叉使用空间的不同使用群体。农园的景观功能多样性创造了丰富的社区空间，为周边社区居民提供了日常交流的功能；在生态永续思想的指导下，农园也是一处都市中的自然学校，为钢筋水泥出生的孩子们打造一处亲近自然和土地的场所；农园所在的创智天地和周边高校资源为农园打造知识型社区提供了文化基底，学术沙龙、自然笔记、社区音乐会等丰富的文化活动又为社区注入新鲜的血液。

园区内部大型企业的社会责任部门与街道推进社会建设和社区治理的自治办在创智农园运营初期给予了很大的帮助，在空间共享、资源互补上加大了交流合

small and focus on personalizing the space and relating it to the residents' lives, giving the residents more ownership of the space and room to change the space in the future. The design team had to have the confidence and patience to look at the garden from the residents' standpoint and communicate with residents to find a plan that would best aid and satisfy them.

The residents, who had almost no prior experience in landscaping, built Baicao Garden in less than one week. Through multiple well-organized, content-rich events, a child-volunteer team was assembled to take responsibility for the daily maintenance of the garden. These activities deepened the children's understanding of personal duty to community and society, and the child-volunteer team has become a dynamic force for community building and garden management. In addition, Baicao Garden also worked with Dahushan Road Primary School as its nature education base, and shared resources with Fun Garden at Anshan 363 Alley, bringing neighboring groups closer together.

The original goal of the community garden was to establish exactly this kind of shared learning mechanism and to turn the space into a "learning garden." The program encouraged the residents to start with small actions, and gradually transformed them from consumers of the garden into active participants and producers. A mark of maturity for a self-governing community garden is whether or not it has a public organization capable of managing the space independently. The greater the number of clubs and events, and the more standardized the management systems are, the more inclusivity and greater levels of resident engagement a garden enjoys. The Baicao Garden explores ways of improving spaces within older and clearly defined residential communities in Shanghai in order to provide new thinking and management models for similar high-density communities with aging residents and further barriers for landscape improvements.

The second case, the Knowledge and Innovation Community Garden (KICG), was established adjacent to Wujiaochang Business District, Shanghai, in a location that was

previously used for temporary housing for construction-site workers. KICG is the first community garden located in an open neighborhood of Shanghai,[1] which was designed as a "community interaction" and recreation space with support from private enterprise.[2] With the guidance of principles of ecological sustainability—including the avoidance of pesticides and chemical fertilizers—KICG also serves as a natural "school" in the city, creating a place close to nature for what is known in China as "reinforced concrete-born" children. The KIC [Industrial] Park and surrounding university resources provide a cultural base for building knowledge-based communities in KICG. Rich cultural activities such as academic salons and community concerts inject fresh life into the community.

Within KICG, social responsibility departments of large enterprises and the self-governance office of the neighborhood responsible for promoting social construction and community governance offered great help in the early stages of operation. They also strengthened exchanges and cooperation regarding space sharing and resource

作。农园定期举办的讲座沙龙，农夫市集，政企合作公益项目和党建团建活动等都离不开政府和企业的支持[3]。

开放街区中的社区花园，周边人口构成更为多元丰富，利益矛盾点也更突出，管理内容较为复杂，需要依靠良好的运行机制和长期实践来培养参与者的自治意识。这类社区花园营造的主要策略是促进多方对话，搭建政府、企业、高校、社会组织和居民多方参与的平台，为合作打下基础。

基于团队近年完成的两个具有代表性的项目创智农园和百草园，从"公"与"私"的两个分类阐述了社区花园营建的过程中各自阶段的特征，以及对应的策略。实践总结，社区边界越模糊，人口构成越复杂，社区花园内容越丰富，营建之初的参与度越低，反之亦然。已经拥有熟人社区环境的居民可以在专业的设计团队指导下全过程地参与到社区花园的营建中，而缺少熟人社区环境的社区则需要设计团队的主导建设一个花园空间，通过运营团队长时间的社区交流、社区活动来帮助建立彼此之间的信任与关系，在之后的管理维护甚至空间更新中逐渐提高居民的参与性。两种模式殊途同归，在建造运营的

初期的策略需要结合各个社区的特性，不同的阶段有不同的处理方式，但两种类型的社区花园目标都是让更多的居民开始关注到身边的环境，开始有意愿有能力有规则地参与到公众事务中，在公众参与的过程中形成自组织，实现共建空间的可持续发展机制。

中国大城市的快速发展带来了不同领域的挑战，要求多学科的交融共同探讨应对城市问题的策略。上海的社区花园作为社区民众以共建共享的方式进行园艺活动的场地，基于景观设计学，连接了社会学、教育学等多学科研究成果来处理人与环境的关系。社区花园是为了实现在上海这样一个高密度人口的城市中能源可持续、社区睦邻友好、自然教育而建立的一次科学的尝试。去除学术的外壳，空间本质上的核心就是人，不仅仅是儿童和老年人，还有年轻人，站在使用人群的角度，关注他们所关注的话题，通过满足他们价值的活动来实现人与人之间的相互连接，使人们对空间产生情感，这才是社区花园背后有生命力的关键所在。

complementarity. The government and enterprises have provided key support to KICG's regular activities including a farmers' market featuring organic food for urban-rural mutual assistance, public welfare programs jointly sponsored by the government and enterprises,[3] as well as activities for Party building and League building.

For community gardens built in open blocks, such as KICG, conflicts of interest can be more noticeable due to the more diversified population mix around them. Our research has found that the key to addressing such conflicts lies in encouraging dialogue among stakeholders, which lays a foundation for cooperation by establishing a platform that involves government agencies, businesses, colleges and universities, social organizations, and local residents.

These two representative projects—Baicao Garden and KICG—expound the main characteristics and corresponding strategies of community garden-building from the different perspectives of "public" and "private." Experience indicates that the degree of participation is lower at the beginning in communities with vague boundaries, a complex population mix, and richer contents of community gardens, and vice versa. Residents in closer relationships to the garden space fully participate in the building of community gardens under the guidance of a professional design team. Residents without such a relationship generally rely more heavily on the design team to plan and build the garden. Ideally, in the latter case, trust and closer relationships should be established through long-term community exchanges and activities managed by the operation team, so that residents' participation can be enhanced in respect of future management, maintenance, and even spatial updating of gardens. Strategies in the early stages of garden building and operation should give consideration to the characteristics of different communities. Solutions should also vary in different stages as well. In fact, despite their differences, both types of community gardens aim to encourage more residents to pay attention to the surrounding environment and properly participate in public affairs with purpose and ability. In the process of public participation, a self-governance organization should be formed to help build a sustainable development mechanism for public space.

The rapid development of metropolises in China brings many challenges. This requires solutions based on interdisciplinary collaborations. As a space for residents to participate in gardening activities through construction and sharing, Shanghai's community gardens are centered on landscape architectural design to deal with human–environment relationships by combining ideas from sociology, education, and other sciences. Community gardens are a scientific attempt to realize sustainable ecosystems, harmonious neighborhood relations, and nature-education activities in a densely populated metropolis like Shanghai. The idea of community gardens is to understand the position of the users, paying attention to their concerns, and arranging activities that meet the community's pursuit of value, promote the interconnection between residents, and enhance people's attachment to place.

1. Liu, Y. et al., "New Approaches to Community Garden Practices in High-density High-rise Urban Areas: A Case Study of Shanghai KIC Garden," *Shanghai Urban Planning Review*, no. 2 (2017): 29–33.
2. Knowledge and Innovation Community of the Shanghai Yangpu Science and Technology Innovation Group Company Limited and the Shui On Group, Yangpu District, Shanghai.
3. For example, in the Love for Children of the Stars initiative organized by the office of Shanghai Landscaping Committee and Green Shanghai Special Fund of China Green Foundation, autistic children, accompanied by their parents, are guided by KICG employees to identify plants and participate in experiments of fostering aquatic plants. The organizers have tried to understand the world from these children's perspectives yet also have left some space for them to think and explore, expecting that their inner potential might be unleashed.

# Landscape: From Aesthetic Experience to Public Health
## 风景：从宜人感受到公共健康

**陈筝** | CHEN Zheng

Associate Professor, Department of Landscape Architecture, Tongji University. Chen holds a bachelor in landscape architecture and a master's in urban planning from Tongji University, as well as a doctorate degree in architecture and design research from Virginia Tech. Her current research involves environmental cognition and its application to enhancing well-being via built environmental design. Chen has had two research projects funded by the Chinese National Science Foundation, and has published over 20 journal articles and one book.

同济大学景观学系副教授，她主要从事环境心理导向的空间规划设计，具体包括基于可穿戴生物传感器（如脑电、皮电、肌电等）的环境感受诊断，和健康促进、体验增强、认知增强的空间交互循证设计。主持中国自然科学基金2项，发表期刊文章20余篇，著作1本。同济大学景观学系本硕、美国佛吉尼亚理工大学建筑及设计研究博士。

Landscape in China is never only about environment in an objective sense. It is a subjective and affective interpretation of natural and built environments.[1] The affective landscape experience is about aesthetics, which is one of the core values of landscape architecture practice and academia.[2] Environmental psychologists have found that affective experience, though complex and implicit, could be simplified into a two-dimensional quantifiable model of valence and arousal.[3] Valence measures the affective preference from pleasant to unpleasant, while arousal measures the intensity of affective responses from weak to strong. Psychologists of emotions found that the two dimensions can be fairly predicted via regression by physiological indicators, such as skin conductance, electrocardiography, electroencephalogram, and facial expression electromyogram.[4] Picard from MIT media lab upgraded the regression predicting method into an affective computing method via machine learning, which increased the predictive accuracy from 50~60% to 80~90%.[5]

Environmental design researchers introduced the physiological approaches to measure the in-situ affective responses to real-time outdoor environment stimuli, which yielded promising preliminary results. Two German research groups measured affective experience within environments via portable sensors. They found that skin conductance was a good predictor of stress responses in a walking or cycling tour, which effectively identified that waterfront streets triggered high pleasure and less stress.[6] An English research group measured the experience of walking across different environments via a portable electroencephalogram device, which revealed that walking through open green spaces would trigger a more peaceful and pleasant experience compared with urban built areas.[7]

Our research measured geo-tagged multi-sensory indicators of real-time environmental experience. The bio-sensory measures we collected include skin conductance, electrocardiography, electroencephalogram, facial expression electromyogram, and respiration, which were synchronized with real-time geo-locations via a GPS device during the walk experience. The computed sensory results were compared against results from an environmental preference Liket Scale and from a labelled experience interview. The preliminary results indicated that the experience can be fairly measured by bio-sensory techniques.[8] Based on the affective stimuli and their locations identified by the bio-sensory technique, we proposed design strategies such as reorganizing pedestrian and parking areas, improving entrance design, and adding more sitting areas.[9]

Notably, pleasant and unpleasant environments may trigger different neural and cognitive processes, which would result in different long-term mental consequences. A survey that we conducted on park use in Shanghai revealed that contacts with nature and parks promote positive public emotional health.[10] We examined the use of four parks during weekends (participants=296), and analyzed the length of time spent in parks per day and its correlation with mental and physical health. After controlling users' personality and social routines (r2=29.22%), more time spent in parks was found to contribute to mental well-being (⊿r2=2.25%). Path analysis further revealed that more park exposure regulated emotion primarily through reducing negative emotions rather than increasing positive ones. Affective responses, including those to environments, can be understood as two types: one that people like and tend to approach, and the other that people dislike or are afraid of and tend to avoid.[11] The intensity of feelings increases in both types as arousal increases. We found that the two types of affective responses trigger different cognitive processes: pleasant environments

中国意义上的“风景”，不是纯粹客观的 “环境”，而是包括人对自然和建成环境感知的情感体验复合体[1]。这种以审美愉悦感为核心的景观情绪感受，无论中美，一直被普遍认为是风景园林学科的核心价值之一，也是行业的核心问题之一[2]。

尽管风景诱发的情绪体验看上去隐晦而复杂，但是环境心理学家发现用情绪效价(valence)和情绪唤醒(arousal)的二维量化模型可以较好地简化描述大部分环境情绪体验[3]。其中情绪效价描述了从宜人到不宜人的环境情感偏好，而情绪唤醒描述了从平静到强烈的情感强烈程度。研究情绪的心理学家通过大量的照片刺激实验，进一步发现情绪模型的两个维度可以较好地通过皮电、心电、脑电、表情肌肌电等生理信号反映，其电信号单因子回归模型能较好地预测两个情绪维度[4]。麻省理工学院媒体实验室的皮卡德教授进一步在此基础上提出情感计算(affective computing)技术，结合机器学习将模型预测准确率从50~60%左右提升到80~90%[5]。

环境设计学者将上述情绪体验生理测量方法引入户外实验，以测量环境使用者对实景空间环境的实时反应，表现出较好的初步效果。两组德国学者用便携仪器记录实时环境体验，发现皮电能较好地捕捉行走或骑行过程中的紧张情绪[6]，并有效识别出宜人性更高、压力更低的滨河道路。一组英国学者采用便携式脑电仪记录穿越不同环境的行走体验，其间穿越开放绿地较穿越城市建成区有更明显的平静宜人感受[7]。

我们进行了结合空间定位的多生理指标实时环境体验测量，其实验结果得到了传统方法研究结果的佐证。我们利用可穿戴传感器采集皮电、心电、脑电、表情肌肌电、呼吸等多项生理指标，结合GPS实时地理追踪，对实景环境行走情绪体验进行实时记录。通过同目前环境视觉体验研究主流应用的莱克特偏好量表问卷[9]和标签式体验访谈的结果对比，发现组合的生理指标能够较好地反映实景情绪体验[8]。针对具体的刺激源及其原因，我们有针对性地提出了设计改进策略，比如改进交通步行流线，强化入口提示，增加停驻休憩设施等等[9]。

值得注意的是，宜人和不宜人的环境应激会诱发不同的神经认知过程，并造成非常不同的心理健康影响。我们就上海市公园使用的调研显示接触自然和公园可以促进公共情绪健康[10]。研究通过上海市区四个公园周末使用者的问卷调查(n=296),考察了日均公园活动时间和情绪、生理健康的关系。在控制人格和社交两大主要因素后(r2=29.22%),日均去公园的时间长短也会一定程度促进人们的情绪健康(⊿r2=2.25%)。在此基础上,路径分析进一步发现公园的这种调节作用主要反映在对负面情绪的调节上,而非对正面情绪的促进上。环境情绪应激可以被分为两大类5:一类是人们喜欢想追求的;另一类是人们厌恶害怕想避开的[11]。随着唤醒强度的增加,两类应激在在效价喜恶上的差异越发明显。在环境认知中,我们发现情绪应激对应的环境感受有不同的加工机制:宜人环境易诱发恢复加工,而不宜人环境易诱发低效率加工。更多心理研究显示正负情绪的长期累积会导致完全不同的影响效果,应当作为两个不同的变量处理[12]。

证据显示风景优美程度可能比自然绿化对健康的影响更为直接。一项研究通过对英国社媒网站Scenic-Or-Not上150万条风景度评价数据结合公共健康统计数据分析,在控制社会经济因素后发现生活在风景优美地区的居民有更好的健康状态[13]。研究同时发现风景度对健康的影响可能比绿化覆盖率还更加显著。综上所述,创造优美宜人的风景环境,对于建设美丽中国、改善居民健康有着积极重要作用,是当代中国风景园林师不可推卸的使命。

may evoke attention and affective restoration while unpleasant environments may evoke inefficient cognitive processes. Accumulative positive and negative responses, as revealed by well-being psychological studies, result in quite different results, which would suggest they be treated as two variables.[12]

Evidence suggested that scenic quality may have a more direct impact on well-being than naturalness. Crowdsourcing data of 1.5 million subjective scenic quality rating votes collected from British social media company Scenic-Or-Not, combined with public health statistics, revealed that people living in scenic places reported better health after controlling social-economic factors.[13] The study also revealed that the association between health and scenic quality was much more significant than that between health and naturalness. The Beautiful China movement offers the current generation of Chinese landscape architects an opportunity to contribute to better human health outcomes by restoring and building beautiful landscapes.

1. Yang R., "Meanings of 'Feng Jing'," *Chinese Landscape Architecture* 9 no. 5 (2010).
2. Liu B., "Trialism – the Philosophical Basis for Studies of Human Inhabitation Environment," *Planners* 15, no. 2 (1999): 81–84; Fein A., *A Study of the Profession of Landscape Architecture* (Princeton: The Gallup Organization, Inc, 1972).
3. Russell J.A. & Snodgrass J., "Emotion and the Environment," In D. Stokols & I. Altman (eds), *Handbook of Environmental Psychology*, vol. 1, (New York: Wiley, 1987) 245–81.
4. Lang P.J., "The Emotion Probe: Studies of motivation and attention," *American Psychology* 50, no. 5 (1995): 372–85; Lang P.J., et al., "Looking at Pictures: Affective, facial, visceral, and behavioral reactions," *Psychophysiology* 30 (1993): 261.
5. Picard R.W., *Affective Computing* (Cambridge, MA: MIT Press, 1997).
6. Bergner B.S., et.al., *Human Sensory Assessment Methods in Urban Planning – a Case Study in Alexandria,* paper presented at Real Corp 2013, Rome, Italy; Höffken S., et al., *EmoCycling – Analysen von Radwegen mittels Humansensorik und Wearable Computing,* paper presented at Real Corp 2014, Vienna, Austria.
7. Aspinall P., et al., "The Urban Brain: Analysing outdoor physical activity with mobile EEG," *British Journal of Sports Medicine* (2013): 1–6.
8. Chen Z. & Liu S., "Real-time Environmental Affective Experience Assessment via Wearable Sensors," *Chinese Landscape Architecture* 34, no. 3 (2018): 5–11.
9. Ibid.
10. Chen, Z., et al., "A Study of the Use Impact of Urban Parks on the Public Health in Shanghai," *Landscape Architecture* 9 (2017): 99–105.
11. Lang P.J., "The Emotion Probe," Ibid.
12. Diener E., et al., "Subjective Well-being: Three decades of progress," *Psychological Bulletin* 125, no. 2 (1999): 276.
13. Seresinhe C.I., Preis T. & Moat H.S., "Quantifying the Impact of Scenic Environments on Health," *Scientific Reports* 5 (2015): 16899.

# Healing Landscape and Beautiful China
## 康养景观与美丽中国

**史舒琳 | SHI Shulin**

Assistant Professor, Landscape Architecture, Technological and Higher Education Institute of Hong Kong. Shi graduated from Tsinghua University, Beijing, with a Bachelor of Architecture and a Master of Engineering in Landscape Architecture, and further obtained her PhD in Landscape Architecture from The University of Hong Kong. Her research and practice mainly focuses on promoting users' well-being with landscape planning and design, evidence-based landscape design, and traditional Chinese landscape architecture.

博士，香港高等教育科技学院（THEi）园境建筑学专业任助理教授。史博士早年于清华大学获建筑学学士及工学硕士（风景园林），后于香港大学获哲学博士（园境建筑）学位。她的科研和实践工作主要关注康养景观规划设计，风景园林循证设计以及中国古典园林。

The call to build a Beautiful China, toward a new era of ecological civilization, is a vision of harmony between humanity and nature. To realize this vision, we need to proactively establish a close and deep connection with nature. According to the biophilia hypothesis,[1] human beings have an innate preference for green spaces, especially in urban contexts.[2] More and more research finds positive changes to the physical, mental, and social well-being of people after contact with nature-dominant places.[3] Consequently, design projects are increasingly exploring landscape's healing potential and its benefit to users' health and well-being.[4]

Our research on gardens in elderly care facilities in Hong Kong also confirms benefits from contact with nature, although the actual outcomes may vary significantly upon different ways and extents of user–garden connections. We have studied the gardens in two independent elderly care facilities in Hong Kong, conducting interviews with 37 residents and 27 staff in total, and observing each garden for two days to study actual usage and solicit users' feedback on the gardens.[5]

The garden in facility 1 is quite large (8,850 m2) designed by a professional landscape architectural consultancy. It is managed by the facility in a similar way to public parks in Hong Kong; that is, users are advised not to touch plants or water features, except in the gardening area. During interviews at this facility, garden users generally categorized the garden into usable paved areas and unusable areas with natural elements. Although all users claimed that they liked to stay in natural environments and considered this beneficial to their well-being, during the two days of observations only 21 user-garden interactions were recorded where users watched the plants or fish. This is only 7% of all 292 user-garden interactions recorded in this garden. Our study found there was little self-initiated interaction between users and garden elements besides organized activities. Even though there were quite a lot of flowering and fragrant plants in the garden, most elderly residents interviewed still suggested to have more flowering plants in the garden. These interviews clearly indicated limited connection between these garden users and natural elements in the garden of facility 1.

On the other hand, the garden in facility 2 is quite small (160 m2), and has been set up by the staff. It is quite open with little restriction on activities. During the two days of observations, a total of 110 user-garden interactions were recorded. There were much more self-initiated uses than facility 1: 55 out of 110 uses involved watching and touching plants (50%), five uses involved cleaning the garden (4.5%), and three uses involved taking care of plants (2.7%). Most interviewed subjects expressed excitement and familiarity when talking about the plants and their growth in the garden, together with appreciation of, and even attachment to, the garden.

According to the results of interviews and observations, there are significant differences in terms of garden perception and usage, as well as well-being benefits between the gardens in these two facilities. One significant difference is found in the respective garden-management regimes of the facilities. The garden management in facility 1 pushes users away from landscape elements physically and mentally, and fails to establish effective connections between them, although the landscape is professionally designed. On the other hand, even though the garden in facility 2 is not designed by professionals, its welcoming management effectively brings users and natural elements together. Thus the garden improves users' well-being and even becomes a key component in their psychological sustenance.

建设美丽中国，走向生态文明新时代的提出，为中国指明了前进方向，对人与自然和谐发展设定了美好的愿景。为了实现这个理想，我们需要主动地与自然建立紧密、深刻的联结。根据亲生命假说（biophilia hypothesis）[1]，人对自然要素具有出于本能的偏好与依赖。此假设不断得到科学研究的支持[2]。更进一步地，越来越多的研究证实不同的使用者在接触以自然要素为主的空间环境后体验到生理、心理及社会交往等方面健康状况的改善[3]。基于这些理论与论据，近年来越来愈多的设计项目引入康养景观的概念，希望利用自然要素改善使用者的健康状况[4]。

笔者基于庭院的研究显示，自然要素对健康的裨益确实存在，但具体效果却可能因使用者与庭院的联结方式和程度不同而大相径庭。笔者早前在香港选取了两间有独立庭院的安老院，全面了解庭院的设计要素和活动项目后，调研院友和职员对庭院的实际使用情况及相关反馈。我们一共访问了37位院友及27位职员，并对每个庭院进行了两天的观察[5]。

安老院1的庭院较大，由专业景观公司设计，采用“公园式”管理，除了园艺种植活动区外，植物和水景等自然要素都只能看，不能动。在访谈中，我们发现庭院在被访者眼中大致分为可以使用的铺装空间和不能使用的自然要素空间。虽然他们都表示喜欢待在自然环境中，且认为这样对自身的健康有益，两天的观察只记录到21人次观赏植物和鱼，仅占全部292人次庭院使用的7%。在院舍组织的活动之外，几乎没有使用者自发地与庭院要素互动。即便庭院中已经种植了许多观花及芳香植物，绝大部分被访的老年院友仍然希望多种植一些花卉植物。这恰恰说明了他们并未与庭院以及其中的自然要素建立紧密或深刻的联系。

安老院2的庭院较小，由院舍职员布置，采用开放式管理，不限制庭院中的活动。两天的观察中，我们共记录了110人次使用庭院，但其中自发与庭院要素的互动远多于安老院1，如观赏、抚摸植物55人次（50%），打扫庭院5人次（4.5%），打理植物等园艺活动3人次（2.7%）等。大部分被访者谈及庭院中植物及其生长情况时都明显表现出对庭院的喜爱与赞赏，甚至依恋。

从访谈和观察的结果来看，两间安老院庭院的感知和使用情况，以及庭院对使用者健康的帮助存在巨大差异。经过分析，笔者认为主要原因在于不同的庭院管理方式。庭院1虽然有专业的景观设计，管理方式却造成使用者和景观要素从心理到物理层面的疏离，没能在二者之间建立有效的联结；庭院2虽然缺乏专业景观设计的支撑，具有亲和力的管理方式却有效拉近了使用者和自然要素的距离，在互动中潜移默化地改善使用者的健康状况，甚至为他们提供心理寄托。

此外，安老院中的院友由于年龄和健康关系往往对职员有较大的依赖。因此，职员对户外活动的认知也会影响院友对庭院的使用。在研究过程中，笔者发现安老院1受访的大部分职员对户外活动有一定的抵触心理，过分强调高温日晒、蚊虫叮咬等问题。同时，他们也不甚了解自然要素对人健康的益处。有鉴于此，笔者在调研结束后为此间安老院的职员进行了一次康养景观科普分享，并引导他们亲身感受庭院里的各种要素，同时为他们讲解空间、景观特质。绝大部分参加者在活动结束后都表示自己从未意识到这个庭院有如此多好处，以后会尽量多利用，并鼓励院友善用这些资源，改善健康状况，提高生活品质。

这两个案例对康养景观设计的主要启示在于，当使用者与景观环境建立有效、深入的联结时，景观的康养效果可以得到明显提升。在设计康养景观时，应该将建立人-景联结作为一个重要目标。不仅需要考虑人-景互动的便利性，也要尽量降低景观维护管理的难度，以便实施更具亲和力的管理方式。必要时也需帮助潜在管理者、使用者认识康养景观的运作原理、扫清有碍人-景联结的心理和认知障碍。基于人类亲近自然的本能，相信如此必然能够促进使用者主动地与康养景观建立紧密、深刻的联结，支持美丽中国的建设。

Due to aging and unfavorable health conditions, elderly residents in these facilities can be heavily reliant upon staff, and therefore the staff's perceptions of outdoor activities can affect residents' garden usage. During our investigation, the majority of interviewed staff in facility 1 psychologically resisted working with patients in the garden. They emphasized problems like high temperature and exposure to the sun and insects, and indicated little appreciation or understanding of how natural elements could positively affect people's health. To counter this, after the investigation, we offered the staff in facility 1 a talk about the health benefits of green space and guided them to experience spaces and landscape features in their own garden. Most participants expressed that they were not aware of benefits of this garden before and that they would like to make better use of it in future and encourage elderly residents to use the garden as well for better well-being and quality of life.

The essential inspiration from these two cases is that the health benefits of landscape can be significantly promoted when effective and deep connection is established between users and landscapes. Therefore, establishing effective user–landscape connections should be considered as an important goal when designing healing landscapes. As well as making user–landscape interaction convenient, it is also important to ensure easy maintenance, so as to facilitate a more welcoming garden management regime. Given humanity's innate preference towards nature, I trust that the results of this research can contribute to the establishment of a more proactive and deep connection between users and healing landscapes as a small but important contribution to a more beautiful China.

1. Wilson E.O., *Biophilia* (Cambridge, MA: Harvard University Press, 1984).

2. Laumann K., Gärling T. & Stormark K.M., "Selective Attention and Heart Rate Responses to Natural and Urban Environments," *Journal of Environmental Psychology* 23 no. 2 (2003): 125–34; Ulrich R.S., "Natural Versus Urban Scenes: Some psychophysiological effects," *Environment and Behavior* 13, no. 5 (1981): 523–56; van den Berg A.E., Hartig T. & Staats H., "Preference for Nature in Urbanized Societies: Stress, Restoration, and the Pursuit of Sustainability," *Journal of Social Issues* (2007): 79–96.

3. Felsten G., "Where to Take a Study Break on the College Campus: An attention restoration theory perspective," *Journal of Environmental Psychology* 29, no. 1 (2009): 160-67; Hartig T., et al., "Tracking Restoration in Natural and Urban Field Settings," *Journal of Environmental Psychology* 23, no. 2 (2003): 109–23; Kaplan S., "The Restorative Benefits of Nature: Toward an integrative framework," *Journal of Environmental Psychology* 15, no. 3 (1995): 169–82; Rappe E., Kivelä S.L. & Rita H., "Visiting Outdoor Green Environments Positively Impacts Self-rated Health among Older People in Long-term Care," *Horticultural Technology* 16, no. 1 (2006): 55–59.

4. Cooper-Marcus C. & Sachs N.A., *Therapeutic Landscapes: An evidence-based design approach to designing of healing gardens and restorative outdoor spaces* (Hoboken, NJ: John Wiley and Sons, 2014); Winterbottom, D. & Wagenfeld A., *Therapeutic Gardens*: *Design for healing gardens* (London: Timber Press, 2015).

5. Shi S.L., Tong C.M. & Tao Y.Q., "How Does Spatial Organization of Gardens at Care Facilities for the Elderly Influence UPe patterns: A case study in Hong Kong," *Landscape Research*, in press; Shi S.L., Tong C.M. & Cooper-Marcus C., "What Makes a Garden in an Elderly Care Facility Well Used?" *Landscape Research* (2018).

中国饭

好人家
豆豉

# Market, or Museum?
# 市场亦是博物馆

**何志森 | Jason Zhisen HO**

Curator, urbanist, and educator. Ho holds a Master of Landscape Architecture and PhD from RMIT University, Australia. Since 2014, he has been leading mapping workshops across China, bringing architecture and landscape architecture students to urban villages, street markets, slums, and factories to understand the art of survival and the human side of design.

策展人，城市研究者和背包客教师。他拥有澳大利亚墨尔本皇家理工大学的景观硕士和博士学位。从2014年开始，何志森在中国各大建筑院校开展他的mapping工作坊，长期和学生一起潜伏在城中村、菜市场、贫民窟、血汗工厂做调研，教导学生理解生存的艺术以及建筑人性的一面。

There is a fresh meat market right next to the FEI gallery, which I am currently working at, in Guangzhou. In 2017, artist Song Dong transformed the concrete separation wall between the meat market and the gallery into a large-scale artwork titled *Borderless Wall*, made of old doors and windows from Beijing's destroyed hutong houses, along with 36 old-style beds and 216 stools. In order to welcome locals, the gallery initiated a series of bed-related community activities and art events, such as having hotpot picnics and watching movies on the beds. Prior to this, the local residents rarely visited the gallery and many knew nothing of its existence. However, eventually, the bed-related activities and events made the gallery visible and accessible to the local residents.

Despite the influx of locals, the vendors working next door in the market still showed no interest in the events and were not willing to visit the gallery. What does the gallery really mean to them? Isn't the market itself already a living gallery? Keeping these questions in mind, I initiated the "Market, or Museum?" workshop with 10 landscape architecture students from the School of Architecture at South China University of Technology.

I started thinking about what I could do and what I couldn't do, or couldn't do simply and crudely. Mostly designers think about how to transform a site spatially, but this can lead to excessive design which turns the real-life scene into

an Instagram picture spot. When designed in this manner, there is a danger that market-stall rents will increase, and consequently so will the price of food. Eventually, the market will be "beautified" and lose its original customers. So, I asked my students to observe the daily lives of the vendors, to live and work with them, to put themselves into their shoes, to become them.

For the first two months, the vendors did not welcome the students. They felt that we were interrupting business and making use of them. The ice-breaking moment appeared on May 2, 2018, when a storm in Guangzhou caused heavy flooding in the marketspace. While most of the students did not show up because of the storm, there was one student, Ma, who persisted going to the market and helped the vendors to save their goods from water damage. From that day on, the attitude of the vendors changed and they began to embrace the students and respond to their questions sincerely.

The students then started collecting stories from the vendors to better understand their lives. Gradually, we noticed that

我在广州工作的地方扉美术馆的左边是一个菜市场。2017年，艺术家宋冬老师用胡同里的废弃门窗在菜市场与美术馆之间做了一个无界的墙，当围墙建起来之后，这部分也变成了我们的美术馆。宋冬老师留下了36张床与216张凳子，为了吸引周边的居民，我们在这些床上组织了很多的活动，比如说吃饭、打边炉，野餐等。之前我们的美术馆是没有居民来的，因为他们往往觉得艺术过于抽象难懂，跟他们的生活无关。但最终，依靠这些与床相关的活动，美术馆和其中展出的艺术作品渐渐成为居民生活中可见与可达的一部分。

但是我们逐渐发现了一个问题，居民都来了，那为什么一墙之隔的菜市场的摊主们还不来？美术馆对他们来说意味着什么呢？难道菜市场本身不就是一个生活的展览馆吗？因此，我想做一些事情。于是我将华南理工大学的10个景观系学生带到了这里来完成菜市场改造的课程。

当我和学生们开始调研时，我开始想什么事我可以做，或者什么事我不能做，或不能简单粗暴地做。很多时候，我们一到场地就想改造他们，而过度的设计往往使得真实的生活场景变成一个网红打卡点。时间一久，菜市

vendors often mentioned their hands when telling stories. According to them, their hands are their most important tools – their lives have been slowly etched into them over time. For instance, one vendor's fingers had become callused from handling eggs for over 20 years; a seafood vendor's hands appeared pale and swollen because of constant daily contact with ice water and fish; and some vendors wore agate bracelets in the belief that agate can help to overcome humidity.

When we go to the market, most of the time we only see the purchases the vendors pass to us; we never pay attention to their hands. These hands are full of stories, some filled with scars and some with love. In their hearts, the vendors may feel that they are menial and forgotten by the public, but their stories revealed that their hands are the proudest parts of their bodies; they each raised their families with a pair of hardworking hands. Their hands become their identity. I therefore encouraged the landscape architecture students to record the hands of the vendors through a series of photographs.

As a final review for the workshop we curated an exhibition of photographs of the hands of 44 vendors along Song Dong's Borderless Wall. On the day it opened, a seafood vendor came to the gallery entrance. She stood there cautiously, for fear of bringing market dirt into the gallery space. She told me from far away that she wanted to come in to "look for her hands." This was one of the most memorable moments in my life; in the past 11 years, we'd never seen a single vendor come to the gallery. Finally we had made an exhibition that was connected to their lives.

On the day of the exhibition's dismantling, the vendors asked for the photos of their hands to be taken back and began to set up their own exhibition in the market. They put their photos purposely next to their business licenses. This was another moment. For vendors, a business license appeared to be particularly abstract, a formal identity given by authorities. The photos of their hands became a more "human" expression of their identities. This empowered them to recognize and celebrate their identities. The business license now becomes the image of their hands.

场租金提高，菜价大涨，最终菜市场会失去他们原本的客户，这便成为了一个绅士化的现象。于是，我让我的学生们先去观察摊贩们的生活，跟他们一起生活和工作，将自己代入他们的生活。

其实在刚开始的两个月，摊贩是不接受学生们的，他们觉得我们是在侵略他们，消费他们。事情的转折点发生在2018年5月2号，广州发生了一场暴雨，美术馆和菜市场都被淹了。当大部分学生都因为下雨没去的时候，有一个学生，小马，还是坚持到菜市场调研，并帮助摊贩搬各种各样的货物。从那一天起，摊贩们对学生的态度转变了，他们把学生们真正当成了他们的一份子。

我们便开始去收集摊贩的故事，了解他们的生活。慢慢我们发现，摊贩们在讲故事的时候，常常会提起他们的手。手，成为了承载他们故事的最重要的载体。 有一个摊贩的手上有鸡蛋茧，是因为长期摸鸡蛋而长出来的。因为摸鸡蛋而摸出茧来，是我们的学生闻所未闻的。有一个海鲜档的摊贩，他的手每一天都因为接触水和杀鱼而浮肿，破皮。有一个卖菜小贩，她有很多的首饰在手上，有戒指，有手镯。其中有一个是她老公送的手链。这是个用玛瑙做的手链，因为广州很潮，他相信这个可以驱寒。

然而，当我们去菜市场的时候，我们大部分时候看到的都是手上的菜，从来不会去留意他们的手。他们的每一双手都充满故事，有一些刻满伤痕，有些充满着爱。在摊贩们的心中，他们往往觉得自己是卑微的，这是大众给他们的一个烙印。但在他们的故事中，手却是他们身体上最骄傲的部位，他们用一双勤劳的手创造了他们的生活。因此，我鼓励学生通过一系列的照片去记录摊贩们的手。

在课程结束汇报时，我们在宋冬无界的墙上展出纪录了44个摊贩的手的摄影作品。在那一天，有一个海鲜摊贩来到了美术馆。她小心翼翼的站在门口，生怕弄脏美术馆的地板。她远远的告诉我说她想“找她的手”。这一刻，成为了我一生中最难忘的一个瞬间，这十一年来，我们在美术馆办了很多的展，从来没有一个摊贩来过，但这一个摊贩，因为她的一双手，她踏进了她十一年来从未踏入的一个美术馆，只因为这个展览与她的生活有关。

在撤展的那一天，摊贩们主动要求希望把他们手的照片领回去，领回去之后，他们开始自主的在菜市场里布展，他们把自己手的照片放在了他们的营业执照旁边。对于摊贩们来说，营业执照是一个特别抽象地、自上而下的一个身份的认同。为了营业执照，他们每个月要多交很多钱，使他们变成真正意义上合法的摊主。而手，却是他们特别特别具体的，充满真实的一个标志。这种真实，给予了他们一个新的对自己的身份的认同，一双骄傲的手就是他最真实的营业执照。

很多景观设计师喜欢把社区美化工程称之为"社区营造"，挑选几个社区居民和设计师一起工作叫"参与式设计"或"社会设计"，让中产阶级群体一起集体自嗨说成是修复"人与人的关联"。然而，这些美丽的词语常常沦落为社区士绅化的帮凶。作为设计师，我们不一定就是要设计这些有形的空间，我们也可以设计人跟人之间的关系，这个菜市场，我们并没有触碰菜市场原本破旧的物理空间，而是通过一种非常柔软的艺术介入甚至是不造物的方式来重新构建摊贩们生而为人的尊严和自信。而我认为这正是美丽中国城市更新和社区营造的成功中最重要的一步。

Many landscape architects in China claim that community renovation or beautification projects are a form of community empowerment. Designers work with several community members, often chosen by them, and they call it "community participatory design" or "social engagement." However, these terms are becoming accomplices to gentrification. As landscape architects, we don't have to physically design these spaces, rather, we can catalyze or create relationships. In the case of the market project, we did not touch the original dilapidated physical space, but through very light interventions we have reconstructed the dignity and self-confidence of the ordinary people that work there. And it is this that is required for the success of Beautiful China.

# 後記

# 后记
# Afterword

# Between Sapience and Sentience: Four Remarks in Response to Beautiful China

## 在智性与感性之间：回应“美丽中国”的四点评论

**冯仕达 | Stanislaus FUNG**

Associate Professor and Director of the MPhil-PhD Program in Architecture, Chinese University of Hong Kong. Since 2018, Fung has been a lecturer in landscape architecture at Harvard University Graduate School of Design. His recent writings can be found in the *RIBA Journal* and *Jianzhu Xuebao*.

香港中文大学建筑学副教授、建筑学博士课程主任。2018年起，他开始在哈佛大学设计研究院任教。近期有多篇著作在《英国皇家建筑学会会刊》以及《建筑学报》发表。

**吴洪德 | WU Hongde**

Research Assistant Professor, School of Design, Shanghai Jiao Tong University. Wu's PhD work on the Tiger Hill in Suzhou shows how Chinese placescapes were created without presumptions of modern ideas of space and perspective. His recent writings have appeared in *Shidai Jianzhu* and *Jianzhu Yichan*.

上海交通大学设计学院助理研究员。他在博士期间所做的关于虎丘绘画的研究揭示了在不借助空间和透视的概念的前提下，中国画家是如何发展场所性的绘画的。部分研究成果已在《时代建筑》和《建筑遗产》等专业期刊上发表。

Beautiful China is a political slogan that has emerged in recent years to describe a Chinese national policy to develop an ecological civilization. My friends and colleagues at the University of Pennsylvania and the editors of the present volume have gathered a disparate set of voices to reflect on this policy event and its implications for the discipline of landscape architecture. The history of capitalism shows us that political slogans can sometimes carry meaning for communities, but at other times are merely empty words. It is clear why many American colleagues would be attracted by a bold Chinese slogan advocating an ecological civilization, since national policy and recent political developments in American politics have often been decried for their inadequacies.

In countries where social and political control are fundamental objectives, and in discussions where the parties involved have significantly different assumptions and priorities, the common good of humankind in ecological challenges might provide a common purpose, but our frames of reference are often multiple and inconsistent. In his *Talking to Strangers: What We Should Know About the People We Don't Know*, the American author Malcolm Gladwell has called our attention to ways of engaging strangers that often led to conflict and misunderstandings.[1] Gladwell's book reminds us of the virtue of assuming the genuineness of the strangers' good intentions. On the other hand, as professionals and scholars, we should also take warning from the fantasies of the Parisian intellectuals who were famously infatuated with the promise of the Cultural Revolution.[2] In order for good faith not to degenerate into vacuous pieties, perhaps we should focus instead on the efficacies and operational challenges of national and local initiatives. Too much willingness to compartmentalize discussions of intention, policy, strategy, and case studies and to limit the level of detail of each discussion can result in sloppy thinking, to the detriment of our common purposes. In what follows, we would like to offer four remarks intended to clarify and refocus the stakes involved.

**1.**

In the work of Roger T. Ames on the ontology of thinking in the Confucian tradition, there is a discussion of Chinese terms relating to "knowing" and "thinking" that allow us to articulate a double frame of reference for Beautiful China.[3] Ames argues that Chinese thinking is not "a process of abstract reasoning" but rather a psychosomatic activity which entails "the achievement of a practical result."[4] Thinking is not cognition aimed at examining an objective world of facts but rather a way of actualizing and realizing a world. The Chinese term zhi 知 (to know) is often used interchangeably in classical texts with zhi 智 (wisdom); this indicates the overlapping senses of being knowledgeable and being wise.[5] Thus, the Confucian writer Dong Zhongshu (c. 179–c. 104 BCE) says, "What is it that is called zhi? It is to predict accurately [literally, to speak first and then for events to happen accordingly]. Any person who desires to get rid of certain conducts acts only after prescribing the situation with his zhi. Where one's prescription is correct, he gets his way in what he does and is appropriate in his undertakings. His actions are successful and his name is illustrious…His good fortune reaches to his children and grandchildren, and his beneficence spreads to all of the people."[6] The person who thinks is the person who focuses on situational proprieties, articulates and projects a moral sense, and enjoins the participation of others. In this context, language is not "free speech" about hypothetical situations but rather

"美丽中国"是近年来以国家政策的名义提出、旨在发展生态文明的一句政治口号。笔者在宾夕法尼亚大学的朋友、同仁，暨本书的编辑们汇集了一组不同的论撰，以思考这项政策对景观建筑学学科的潜在意义。资本主义发展史告诉我们，有时候政治口号对社群来说是有意义的；而在其他时候只不过是一种空话。鉴于当下美国国家政策和政治进程的弊端经常受到抨击，也难怪这一大胆倡导生态文明的中国口号会引发美国同仁的关注了。

人类作为一个利益共同体应如何面对生态环保的挑战，为许多复杂情况提供了弥合分歧的共同目标。不仅在以社会、政治管制为根本追求的国家里是这样，在连对话前提和价值标准都莫衷一是的国际讨论中亦然。尽管拥有共同目标，人们思考的参考系往往却是多样的、不一致的。美国作家马尔科姆·格莱德维尔（Malcolm Gladwell）写了一本《与陌生人交谈：关于陌生人的必备知识》，解释哪些打交道方式是容易引起冲突和误解的[1]。这本书也让我们意识到，相信陌生人的善意是能带来益处的。另一方面，作为专业人士和学者，我们也应该从那些迷恋中国文革的法国知识分子中吸取到教训[2]。为了不让善意的假设沦为虔诚空话，也许我们应该关注国家或地方的初衷（initiative）在实践效果、运行状态方面正面临着哪些挑战。过往我们总是将意图、政策、战略和案例研究都割裂成单独话题，乐不知疲地单独讨论。这些讨论各自为政，也不够详细，往往流于表面。于是引发了各种浑水摸鱼的情况，潦草的思考也弱化了我们共同的目标。在接下来的文章中，我们将来澄清和重估此中的风险，分为四点评论。

**1.**

在安乐哲（Roger T. Ames）讨论儒家传统思维本体论的著作里面，有一项关于汉语词汇"知"与"思"的讨论，可以让我们弄清楚"美丽中国"概念中存在的双重参考系[3]。安乐哲认为，中国思维不是"一个抽象推理的过程"，而是一个追求"实际结果"的身心一体的活动[4]。思维的目的不在于认知、审视那个由"事实"构成的客观世界，而在于让世界本身得以具现（actualize）和实现（realize）。古代文献中的"知"和"智"是通假字，这暗示着知识渊博和智慧充盈二者在意义上具有重叠的部分[5]。因此大儒董仲舒说道："何谓之知？先言而后当。凡人欲舍行为，皆以其知，先规而后为之，其规是者，所为得其所事，当其行，

遂其名，荣其身，故利而无患，福及子孙，德加万民，汤武是也……[6]”思考者因地制宜(situational proprieties)，他阐明并宣扬守义合宜的道德意识，也鼓动他人的身体力行。以这种语境来看，语言不再是表达假设情况的“自由言说”(free speech)，而是某种有意图的、述行性(performative)的、有预言作用的表达：去“说”就是去“做”，并且也是号召、鼓动他人去做。这种思维的观念并不包含古希腊人“给概念进行严格定义，并将其与实体关联起来”的意思。

因此，我们可以将“美丽中国”理解为这样一种中国式的政治口号：它是一种以模糊观念(而非精确概念)运作的、述行性的话语方式，在后续实践场景的发展过程中，它为进一步自我具体化和个性化预留了空间。在当代中国大陆的语境中，政治口号诉诸于一种对自上而

something purposeful, performative, and predictive: to say is to do, and to enjoin others to do. This notion of thinking does not carry the Greek sense of defining concepts strictly and relating them to actual instances.

In this sense, we can understand Beautiful China as a Chinese political slogan in terms of a kind of performative utterance dealing in vague notions (rather than strict concepts) that leaves much room for further specification and individuation in a ramifying series of contexts. In the contemporary mainland Chinese context, political slogans appeal mostly to an emotive assent in a top-down (i.e., authoritarian) manner and the conceptual and technical apparatuses are often underplayed. Slogans do not come with guarantees about outcomes but they set up

《鹊华秋实图》 赵孟頫

*The Autumn in Que and Hua Mountains* by Zhao Mengfu

a propensity in national development. Individual ministries would position themselves to bid for government funds. Successive levels of government would echo rhetorically the initial slogan and use it to support their claims for funding and to justify their local interests. It is at these intermediate levels of government where, in the absence of an effective correlation of policy and expertise, there might be an uneven commitment among people (not to say outright cynical opportunistic careerists) and varying degrees of strategic cogency.

In a number of thoughtful and engaging essays in this volume, we can see how this plays out in Chinese landscape architectural discussions. Han Feng offers a focused account of the macro-situation that disposes readers to act. She has

下的（权威制的）方式的情感认同，而理念的、技术的建置则往往被轻描淡写一笔带过。口号虽不保证会带来结果，但它们树立了在国家层面进行全面开发的倾向。个别部委会寻找自身的定位，以争取政府的资金。各下级政府也会字斟句酌地响应最初的口号，来为地方财政、或者其他地方利益提出诉求。由于政策和专业领域缺乏有效的互动，正是在这些政府的中等层次中，会出现投入程度不同的情况（更别说存在纯粹的投机行为），以及决策连贯性好坏不一的情况。

在本书几篇引人深思的文章里，可以看到这种话语方式如何在中国景观建筑学引发了各种讨论。韩锋提供了对宏观形势的一种握要的论述，有助于读者据此调整自身行动的部署。她还引入了“深度生态”的想法，回应了为最初的政治口号注入实质内涵的需求[7]。张振威讨论了“美丽中国”制度建设的几个关键方面，让我们了解到口号是如何获得制度力量的[8]。这种工作的潜力在于，它可以帮助大家将来探讨省级及以下的政府是如何面对治理上的挑战的：“上有政策，下有对策”。我们能简单地认为，所谓机遇就仅仅是“国家政策为景观建筑师提供了实践机会”吗？还是应该尝试发展一种更精细的理解：“机遇”事实上体现在自“上面”所出的和自“地方”所出的制度力量的间隙之处。

在本书话语光谱的另一端，何志森、刘悦来（及许俊丽）讨论的小尺度、社区级别的自发性尝试（initiative）显示出，单个项目如何将景观学的专业实践带入基层社会参预的图景里面去[9]。这里还有一个值得将来进一步讨论的关键议题：如何发展对“市民的”自发性尝试的比较研究。就这方面来说，关注过去30年里面国家和社会间一直存在的空隙可能也会带来新的机会，“第三方”机构[10]（大学、非营利组织、民间团体）可以借此在国家和整体的社会之间展开很有效的工作。

**2.**

在题为“作为异化的美学”（Aesthetics as Alienation）的一篇近文中，艺术家戴安·鲍埃尔（Diann Bauer）把美国哲学家罗伯特·布兰顿（Robert Brandom）的一对概念引入了美学的讨论：智性（sapience）和感性（sentience）[11]。两位作者提醒我们注意鹦鹉的行为方式。鹦鹉能从其他颜色中区分出红色的物体来，这一点人类也能做到；但是人类和鹦鹉的认知之间区别何在呢？布兰顿认为，鹦鹉对“红色”的反应是发出吵闹的鸣叫，而人类的反应是“运用概念”[12]。新的语境让两位作者撇开了将智性等同于智慧的传统看法，提出“智性是人类运用概念的能力”。按照他们的理解，感性（sentience）位于智性光谱的另外一端，意味着非概念化的“知”，也即是中国设计师们常说的“感性”。

在上行下效的体制里面，“言”出必“行”。行之前不必再针对具体情境进行必要性、可行性的调研，因此学科的分析性、情景性的考虑往往缺席于决策过程。进而，上层含糊的指令往往引发下层脱离学科概念的即兴回应，这些参差不齐的即兴回应可以说是“感性”而非“智性”的。设想一下，如果生态讨论在经过美丽中国的话题之后，走向了显著的非概念化认知模式，那会发生什么？技术之选和明智之选，两种选择之间的联系会

also responded to the need to give substance to the initial political slogan by introducing the idea of “deep ecology.”[7] Zhang Zhenwei’s essay on the legislative and institutional developments associated with Beautiful China calls our attention to significant aspects of how a slogan takes on regulatory force.[8] This paves the way for a potential exploration of the challenges of governance at provincial and other lower levels of administration: “policies from above call forth counter-policies locally.” Can we simply say that national policy offers opportunities to landscape architects, or should we also try to articulate a finer-grained understanding of the opportunities in the interstices between what comes from “above” and what comes from “the local”?

At the other end of the spectrum, the small-scale, community-level initiatives discussed by Jason Ho and Liu Yuelai (with Xu Junli) show how individual projects can involve landscape architecture in scenarios of grassroots social engagement.[9] Here, a crucial issue that can be taken up in future discussions is the comparative understanding of “civic” initiatives. In this respect, there might be an opportunity to focus on the gap that has emerged between state and society in the past 30 years, where agents of the “third realm”[10] (universities, NGOs, the so-called minjian groups) can work to good effect in between the state and society-at-large.

**2.**

In her recent essay “Aesthetics as Alienation,” the artist Diann Bauer introduced a pair of terms from the American philosopher Robert Brandom into her discussion of aesthetics: sapience and sentience.[11] Bauer and Brandom call attention to the behavior of parrots. Parrots can distinguish red objects from objects of other colors, and so can humans. What, therefore, is the difference between human cognition and the thinking of parrots? Brandom argues that parrots respond to “red” by making noises while humans respond by “applying concepts.”[12] In this context, Bauer and Brandom move away from the traditional link between sapience and wisdom and argue, instead, that “sapience is the human ability to apply concepts." According to their understanding, sentience lies at the other end of the spectrum from sapience and means nonconceptualized knowing, the sort of behavior that Chinese designers might like to call *ganxing* (intuitive). What would happen if discussions of ecology moved via Beautiful China into a predominantly nonconceptualized mode of knowing? Would the links between technical and wise choices be kept out of public discussion? What would happen if overt policy pronouncements using slogans met covert counter-measures as local governments and professionals worked out ways to take advantage of the emerging policy environment? Here we can see the useful sense of sapience in the contemporary context, not as the sagely but vague mobilization of the masses but as the sharp articulation of conceptual distinctions that allows strategies to gain traction in specific scenarios at different scales of thinking. In this sense, we would maintain the probity of academic thinking by not merely promoting "thought leadership" but also asking, for instance, how various sponge cities are, or are not, matched in conception and strategy to the specific scope of administrative jurisdictions. That is, we would ask whether a reasonable distinction can be made between operative sponges and rhetorical ones. We would call the bluff of latter-day Chinese (Confucian) politicians and professionals who assume that to say is to do. We could also maintain the probity of academic thinking by asking when we should insist on quantified data and rational correlation of concepts and cases (for example, in discussions of water reticulation and management of water resources), and when we might not allow a social scientific mentality to lull us into the endless world of small-sample surveys. In sum, we would move away from simplified presentations of "great ideas" and consider the conditions and limits of professional initiatives and their efficacy, real or imagined.

**3.**

As we reviewed the papers in this volume, the sentience (or implicit knowing) of the contributors became evident

被排除在公共讨论之外吗?再设想一下,如果使用口号的显性政策公告最终遇上了地方政府、专业人士的隐性对策(功利地回应了正在形成的政策环境),那又会发生什么?在这样的当代语境中,我们可以看到智性作为一种观念的用处。不是作为神圣却含糊的集体动员令,而是作为对概念差别的敏锐、清晰的区分,它可以在各种尺度的具体思考图景中让策略和实况有效地对应起来。

在这种意义上,我们应当采取各种方式维护学术思考的严肃性。不仅是提倡"思想领导力"而已,而是同时也要按智性的方面考究一下。比如说我们可以考虑各种版本的"海绵城市"是否合适地对应了行政区域的分管机制?换句话说,我们能否区分有效的海绵城市和语言伪术的海绵城市呢?这种发问可能暴露出当下中国(儒家)政客和专业人士所假设的"去说就是去做"的弊端。此外,我们也应当考虑,在哪些情况下,我们应当坚持使用量化数据,或建立概念和案例之间的理性关联(比如在水资源管理和水网系统的讨论中);又在哪种情况下,也许应该避免让社会科学的惯常态度诱使我们不断进行低量样本的调研。总之,要避免以简化的方式来展示"美妙点子"(great ideas)。并考虑专业实践的条件和局限,以及它的(真实或想象的)效果。

**3.**

在回顾本书的各篇论文时,笔者感到,作者们的感性认知可以用四个暗含问题折射出来:

(1) 我们怎样去设想"国家梦想"和学科发展之间的关系,又可以用怎样的实质内容去落实这种关系?
(2) 如何通过概念的准确表达来提高学科的公共性和理性?
(3) 如何利用案例研究来帮助学科发展?
(4) 如何在中国城乡关系的语境中,厘清讨论"美丽乡村"的学术目标?

限于条件,本文未能对这些问题展开详细讨论。读者们可以使用这些问题作为阅读本书论文的指针,或可免于迷失在话题的混杂表象之中。读者们将意会到,目前并没有哪位作者将这些问题明确地提出来,并组成一组议题;然而本书各篇有不少将某一问题作为暗含视域的段落。

in the form of four implied questions that they were engaged with:

(1) In what ways can we imagine and give substance to the relationship between a "national dream" and the development of our discipline?

(2) In what ways can the precise articulation of concepts play a useful role in enhancing the public and rational character of our discipline?

(3) How can case studies assist in the development of our discipline?

(4) In the context of urban–rural relationships in China, how can we articulate the academic purpose of discussing "beautiful villages" in rural and agricultural areas?

The circumstances in which we offer these remarks does not allow us to enter into a detailed discussion of these questions. Each reader can use these questions as pointers to read the essays gathered in this volume and work with what might otherwise appear to be a jumble of voices. It will be evident that no contributor has spelled out these questions explicitly and addressed them as a set. Yet there is no shortage of passages that imply one of the four questions as the horizon of discussion.

In reading the essays in this volume against the four implied questions, we observed how frequently lines of discussion had kept apart considerations that might be brought together usefully. For example, an essay might discuss concrete cases in great detail yet stop short of effectively discussing the broader issues. Other essays might read more or less like manifestos that respond to the initial slogan, but without offering reliable concepts and analysis. Opportunities for cross-cultural discussions are often diminished in these instances. We can also find intriguing attempts to provide post facto justifications for the initial political slogan.

在本书各篇与上述四个暗含问题的对照阅读中，我们发现许多一经组合便能产生效用的思考，但可惜的是经常被讨论的路线隔开了。比如，某篇文章可能细致地讨论了某项实施案例，却没能延伸出对宏观话题的有效讨论。其他一些读起来可能有点像回应最初口号的宣言，却没能使用可靠的概念和分析，以至跨文化讨论的机会也常被消泯掉了。我们也发现了一些为最初的政治口号事后补充理据的有趣尝试。

**4.**

在这种情形下，我们希望提请大家注意一种倾向于提出"宏大关键词"(portentous keywords)的修辞习惯。它仿佛是在要求读者相信，新的关键词意味着新的学科概念或者学科公理。不过我们认为，如果能够追问一下这些新关键词是否挑战了既有的学术预设或者理解，则会对我们的领域大有裨益。换句话说，我们需要看到关键词是否具有分辨力：何者不过是修辞性的新姿态，何者昭示了调整过的新预设、新理解。这有可能鼓励我们将"大想法"和(社区项目的)微观实践放在一起思考，而不必将它们分开。我们可以考虑：二者是否能够在共同预设和理解的基础上统一起来；又或者，作为实践主体的个人是否已经找到了恰当的方式，能够在日常工作与社区参与之间引入新意。

这些或新或旧的关键词能否帮我们确定朱育帆和许愿在文章中提出的基地潜质(potentials)的具体含义[13]？关键词能让感知变得敏锐，从而让潜质显现吗？要消除关键词自身、及其在讨论中角色的含混，一种办法是要区分关键词的种类：有指向资源和环境危机的关键词；也有关于恢复、改进机制的关键词(mechanisms of recuperation and amelioration)；有唤起注意、促进行动、辨识不同路径和可能性的关键词。有些关键词能对应具体的研究方法，可以让我们关注哪些机制在哪些具体情境中起了积极作用，而不用理会乌托邦式的幻想。也存在对关键词的多尺度(multi-scalar)理解，这种关键词系列配上案例研究后，可以为讨论提供更加稳定的参考系。有的关键词是意义开放的，需要依靠案例研究来让意义具体化；换句话说，这些关键词让我们的注意力聚焦到经验和知识之间的反馈环路(feedback loop)上去。在比较随便的闲谈中，感性占了上风，我们往往容易忽略了这种对反馈环路的认识。

总之,“美丽中国”或许为我们开辟了好多条容易跑偏的难行小径:它们徘徊在美学与生态之间,智性与感性之间,公开宣传和潜在迂回之间,需要我们仔细辨识,谨慎前行。

鸣谢:本文原版以英文写成,此处是首次中译。在翻译过程中得到了香港中文大学孙雄先生、哈佛燕京学社王颖博士和华东理工大学潘逸炜先生的帮助,在此表示忱谢。

**4.**

In this context, we would like to call attention to the rhetorical habit of proposing portentous keywords, so that it appears as if readers are asked to believe that new keywords mean new concepts or new axioms for a field. It seems to us that our field would benefit considerably by asking whether new keywords challenge existing assumptions and understandings. In other words, we should see if there is a distinction between a new rhetorical gesture and newly established assumptions and understandings. This might encourage us to think about “big ideas” and micro-practices (of community projects) together rather than separately. We can ask whether they are united by common assumptions or understandings, or whether individuals have found ways to introduce measures of difference into their daily work and community engagements.

Can keywords, new and old, help us focus on the potentials of the sites to which Zhu Yufan and Xu Yuan refer in their essay?[13] Can keywords play a role in stimulating shifts of perception that might reveal potentials? One way to clarify the confusion of keywords and their roles in discussions would be to distinguish between different kinds of keywords. There are keywords that point to contingencies of resource and environment. There are also keywords that deal with mechanisms of recuperation and amelioration. There are keywords that focus attention, prompt us to action, and help us to differentiate between multiple approaches and possibilities. Some of these keywords can be matched with specific techniques of investigation, so that instead of echoing utopian dreams we can focus on situations in which agency was made effective. There is a multi-scalar sense of keywords, and a menu of these keywords articulated to case studies will provide a more stable framework of discussion. There are concepts that are open-ended and depend on case studies for their sense; in other words, these keywords call our attention to the feedback loop between experience and knowledge. This tends to be obscured in casual (suibian) discussions, where sentience is given the upper hand.

In sum, Beautiful China might be opening up for us various slippery paths between aesthetics and ecology, between sapience and sentience, between propaganda and indirection.

1. Gladwell M., *Talking to Strangers: What We Should Know About the People We Don't Know* (New York: Little, Brown and Company, 2019).
2. Wolin R., *The Wind from the East: French Intellectuals, the Cultural Revolution, and the Legacy of the 1960s* (Princeton, NJ: Princeton University Press, 2010).
3. Ames R.T., "Confucius and the Ontology of Knowing," in Larson G.J. & Deutsch E. (eds), *Interpreting Across Boundaries: New Essays in Comparative Philosophy* (Princeton: Princeton University Press, 1988), 265–79.
4. Ibid., 266. On the use of generalizations in cross-cultural comparisons, see Hall D.L. & Ames R.A., *Anticipating China: Thinking Through the Narratives of Chinese and Western Culture* (Albany: State University of New York Press, 1995), xv.
5. Ibid., 267.
6. Ibid., 268. On recent scholarship on Dong Zhongshu, see Major J.S., "Review of Loewe M., *Dong Zhongshu, a 'Confucian' Heritage and the Chunqiu fanlu,*" *China Review International* 19, no. 2 (2012): 302–05.
7. Han F., "The Philosophy behind Beautiful China," in Weller R.J. & Hands T.L., *Beautiful China: Reflections on Landscape Architecture in Contemporary China* (Novato, CA: ORO Editions, 2020), 32.
8. Zhang Z., "Institutional Construction of Beautiful China," ibid., 68.
9. Ho J., "Market, or Museum?" ibid., 188; Liu Y. & Xu J., "Participatory Construction of Public Urban Landscapes," ibid., 168.
10. Huang P.C.C., "'Public Sphere'/'Civic Society' in China? The Third Realm Between State and Society," *Modern China* 19, no. 2 (April 1993); 216–40. Wakeman F., Jr., "The Civil Society and Public Sphere Debate: Western Reflections on Chinese Political Culture," *Modern China* 19, no. 2 (April 1993): 108–38. Zhou L., "Understanding China: A Dialogue with Philip Huang," *Modern China* 45, no. 4 (2019): 392–432.
11. Bauer D., "Aesthetics as Alienation," in Gage M.F. (ed.), *Aesthetics Equals Politics: New Discourses across Art, Architecture, and Philosophy* (Cambridge, MA: MIT Press, 2019), 196–97.
12. Ibid., 197.
13. Zhu Y. & Xu Y., "Toward a Space of Capability," in *Beautiful China*, ibid., 126.

Acknowledgments: For valuable advice on translating the English text into Chinese, the authors would like to thank Mr Sun Xiong (Chinese University of Hong Kong), Dr Wang Ying (Harvard Yenching Institute), and Mr Pan Yiwei (East Chinese University of Science and Technology, Shanghai).

囂與鳴我

# 特别鸣谢
# Credits

# 特别鸣谢 | CREDITS

**篆书题字**
封面与分隔页篆书题字 姚衬多供稿.

**参与建设美丽中国**
英译中, 张晨笛翻译。
p. 14: 英国斯图尔黑得帕, 塔特姆·汉兹拍摄供图, 已获得作者许可。
p. 15:《富春山居图》, 作者黄公望, 公共版权。

**美丽中国与景观学的担当**
中译英, 蔡伊凡翻译。
p. 20–21: 浙江省永嘉县茗岙梯田, 郑盛远拍摄供图, 已获得作者许可。
p. 23: 古代裹脚小鞋, 郑盛远供图, 已获得作者许可。
p. 25: 宿迁三台山衲田花海, 土人景观供图, 已获得作者许可。
p. 27: 三亚红树林生态公园, 土人景观供图, 已获得作者许可。

**美丽中国——融合人与自然, 创建诗意栖居**
中译英, 蔡伊凡翻译。
p. 30–31: 浙江省永嘉县村落, 郑盛远拍摄供图, 已获得作者许可。
p. 33: 江南风光, 郑盛远拍摄供图, 已获得作者许可。
p. 35: 浙江省南山村, 正在劳作的工人们, 严建云拍摄供图, 已获得作者许可。
p. 36: 江南捕鱼, 郑盛远拍摄供图, 已获得作者许可。

**美丽中国人居风景园林观及其现代性转变**
p. 38–39: 苏州老城, 郑盛远拍摄供图, 已获得作者许可。
p. 41: 杭州西湖泛舟, 郑盛远拍摄供图, 已获得作者许可。
p. 43: "风-景"分析图, 刘滨谊绘制, 已获得作者许可。

**山水与人居**
p. 44–45: 浙江杭州西湖鸟瞰图, 郑盛远拍摄供图, 已获得作者许可。
p. 48:《千里江山图》, 作者王希孟, 公共版权。
p. 49:《清明上河图》, 作者张择端, 公共版权。

**图像化"美丽中国"**
p. 52–53: 杭州高铁站, 郑盛远拍摄供图, 已获得作者许可。
p. 55–56: 1958年发行的关于"特-27林业建设"的邮票, 中国邮政, 赵纪军供图。
p. 59: 2016年发行的第二套关于"美丽中国"的邮票, 中国邮政, 赵纪军供图。

**超越美丽**
中译英, 张晨笛翻译。

**Calligraphy**
Original calligraphy by Yao Chenduo.

**Engaging with Beautiful China**
English to Chinese translation by Chendi Zhang.
p. 14: "Stourhead, England" by Tatum Hands, used with permission.
p. 15: *Dwelling in the Fuchun Mountains* by Huang Gongwang, public domain.

**Beautiful China and the Mission of Landscape Architecture**
p. 20–21: "Mingao terraced fields in Yongjia Town, Zhejiang Province" by Shengyuan Zheng, used with permission.
p. 23: "Traditional Chinese shoe" by Shengyuan Zheng, used with permission.
p. 25: "Suqian Santaishan flower quilt" by Turenscape, used with permission.
p. 27: "Sanya Mangrove Park" by Turenscape, used with permission.

**The Philosophy behind Beautiful China**
Chinese to English translation by Yifan Cai.
p. 30–31: "Village in Yongjia Town, Zhejiang Province" by Shengyuan Zheng, used with permission.
p. 33: "Yangtzee River south" by Shengyuan Zheng, used with permission.
p. 35: "Workers in Nanshan Village, Zhejiang Province" by Jianyun Yan, used with permission.
p. 36: "Fishing, Yangtzee River" by Shengyuan Zheng, used with permission.

**Beautiful China: Heaven, Earth, and Humanity**
p. 38–39: "City view of Suzhou old town" by Shengyuan Zheng, used with permission.
p. 41: "Boats on West lake in Hangzhou" by Shengyuan Zheng, used with permission.
p. 43: "Feng Jing diagram" by Liu Binyi, used with permission.

**Landscape and Human Settlement**
p. 44–45: "Aerial view of West Lake in Hangzhou, Zhejiang Province" by Shengyuan Zheng, used with permission.
p. 48: *The Vast Land* by Wang Ximeng, public domain.
p. 49: *Riverside Scene at Qingming Festival* by Zhang Zeduan, public domain.

**Representations of Beautiful China**
p. 52–53: "High Speed Train Station in Hangzhou" by Shengyuan Zheng, used with permission.
p. 55–56: "Stamps depicting forestry development – 1958" by the People's Postal

Service of China, courtesy of Zhao Jijun.
p. 59: "Stamps depicting beautiful China – 2016" by the People's Postal Service of China, courtesy of Zhao Jijun.

**Beyond Beauty**
Chinese to English translation by Chendi Zhang.
p. 60–63: "West Lake in Hangzhou" by Shengyuan Zheng, used with permission.

**Institutional Construction of Beautiful China**
p. 66–67: "Aerial view of Village in Yongjia Town, Zhejiang Province" by Shengyuan Zheng, used with permission.
p. 69: "Laojunshan Mountain" by Zhao Zhicong, courtesy of Zhang Zhenwei, used with permission.
p. 70: "Meilei Snow Mountain" by Zhao Zhicong, courtesy of Zhang Zhenwei, used with permission.

**Seeking Evidence-Based Ecological Practice**
p. 72–73: "Mingao Terraces, Yongjia, Zhejiang Province" by Shengyuan Zheng, used with permission.
p. 75: "Tonglongtan Pool in Yunnan Province" by Xing Kun, used with permission.

**Constructing an Ecological Civilization**
English to Chinese translation by Yifan Cai.
p. 80–81: "Villagers build new home in Yongjia Town, Zhejiang Province" by Shengyuan Zheng, used with permission.
p. 84–87: Images by University of Pennsylvania Weitzman School of Design Jing-Jin-Ji megaregion studio, courtesy of Richard Weller, used with permission.

**The Evolution of China's Polder Landscapes**
p. 92–93: "Polders" by Shengyuan Zheng, used with permission.
p. 95: Historical map of Hangzhou, author unknown, public domain.

**Beautiful Countryside**
p. 98–99: "Fields" by Zhang Jinshi, used with permission.
p. 101: "Typical rural landscape in Handan, Hebei Province" by Zhang Jinshi, used with permission.

**Building Beautiful China: Rural Case Studies**
p. 104–05: "Drying herbs in traditional village, Yongjia, Zhejiang Province" by

p. 60–63: 浙江省杭州市西湖水景风光鸟瞰航拍图，郑盛远拍摄供图，已获得作者许可。

**美丽中国的制度建设**
p. 66–67: 浙江省永嘉县村落鸟瞰图，郑盛远拍摄供图，已获得作者许可。
p. 69: 老君山风光，作者赵智聪，张振威供图，已获得作者许可。
p. 70: 梅里雪山风光，作者赵智聪，张振威供图，已获得作者许可。

**循证生态规划设计**
p. 72–73: 浙江省永嘉县茗岙梯田，郑盛远拍摄供图，已获得作者许可。
p. 75: 云南省通龙潭，邢琨拍摄供图，已获得作者许可。

**建设一种生态文明**
英译中，蔡伊凡翻译。
p. 80–81: 浙江省永嘉县村民盖新房，郑盛远拍摄供图，已获得作者许可。
p. 84–87: 图片来自宾夕法尼亚大学斯图尔特·威兹曼设计学院京津冀超大区域设计课，理查德·韦勒供图，已获得作者许可。

**中国传统圩田景观研究**
p. 92–93: 圩田，郑盛远拍摄供图，已获得作者许可。
p. 95: 杭州历史地图，作者不详，公共版权。

**美丽乡村**
p. 98–99: 田野，张晋石拍摄供图，已获得作者许可。
p. 101: 河北邯郸乡村景观，张晋石拍摄供图，已获得作者许可。

**建设美丽中国：美丽乡村案例研究**
p. 104–05: 浙江省永嘉县传统村落里晾晒草药，郑盛远拍摄供图，已获得作者许可。
p. 107: 大淀头沿河街道景观，张天洁拍摄供图，已获得作者许可。
p. 109: 天津西井峪石磨小品，张天洁拍摄供图，已获得作者许可。

**大棚景观**
中译英，张晨笛翻译。
p. 112–13: 韩涛拍摄供图，已获得作者许可。
p. 115: 上海郊区大棚鸟瞰图，郑盛远拍摄供图，已获得作者许可。
p. 116: 韩涛拍摄供图，已获得作者许可。

**棕地之美**
p. 118–19: 朱育帆工作室拍摄供图，已获得作者许可。

p. 121–22: 郑晓笛拍摄供图, 已获得作者许可。
p. 124: 上海徐汇区滨水公园, 郑盛远拍摄供图, 已获得作者许可。

**走向潜质空间**
中译英, 张晨笛翻译。
p. 126–27: 卓百会拍摄供图, 已获得作者许可。
p. 129: 上海辰山植物园矿坑花园, 朱育帆工作室拍摄供图, 已获得作者许可。
p. 130: 北京首钢矿坑遗址公园, 朱育帆工作室拍摄供图, 已获得作者许可。

**美丽城市**
英译中, 郑盛远翻译。
p. 134: 上海城市天际线, 郑盛远拍摄供图, 已获得作者许可。
p. 137–40: 图片来自宾夕法尼亚大学斯图尔特·威兹曼设计学院京津冀超大区域设计课, 玛丽莲·泰勒供图, 已获得作者许可。

**中国未来公共空间**
英译中, 蔡伊凡翻译。
p. 142–43:上海徐汇区滨水公园篮球活动, 郑盛远拍摄供图, 已获得作者许可。
p. 145: 上海静安寺公园, 郑盛远拍摄供图, 已获得作者许可。
p. 147: 上海田子坊, 郑盛远拍摄供图, 已获得作者许可。
p. 148: 上海街景, 郑盛远拍摄供图, 已获得作者许可。

**公园城市**
p. 152–53: 上海人民公园, 郑盛远拍摄供图, 已获得作者许可。
p. 155: 上海某公园, 郑盛远拍摄供图, 已获得作者许可。
p. 156: 在浙江西湖旁休憩, 郑盛远拍摄供图, 已获得作者许可。

**地被生境实验室**
p. 158–59: 地被生境实验室, 李仓栓拍摄, 刘晖供图, 已获得作者许可。
p. 161: 不同季节里的地被植物群落, 刘晖与李仓栓拍摄供图, 已获得作者许可。
p. 162: 不同季节里的地被植物群落组合模型, 刘晖与李仓栓拍摄供图, 已获得作者许可。

**中国的社区参与式景观营造探索**
p. 166–73: 刘悦来供图, 已获得作者许可。

**风景:从宜人感受到公共健康**
p. 174–75: 上海步行天桥, 郑盛远拍摄供图, 已获得作者许可。

**康养景观与美丽中国**
p. 180–81: 上海徐汇区滨水公园跑步道, 郑盛远拍摄供图, 已获得作者许可。

**市场亦是博物馆**
中译英, 蔡伊凡翻译。
p. 186–90: 何志森供图, 已获得作者许可。

**在智性与感性之间:回应"美丽中国"的四点评论**
p. 196–97: 苏州平江历史街区鸟瞰图, 郑盛远拍摄供图, 已获得作者许可。

Shengyuan Zheng, used with permission.
p. 107: "Waterfront streetscape in Dadiantou Village" by Zhang Tianjie, used with permission.
p. 109: "Millstone in historic Xijingyu Village" by Zhang Tianjie, used with permission.

**XL Greenhouse**
Chinese to English translation by Chendi Zhang.
p. 112–13: Image by Han Tao, used with permission.
p. 115: "Aerial view of greenhouses outside of Shanghai" by Shengyuan Zheng, used with permission.
p. 116: Image by Han Tao, used with permission.

**The Beauty of Brownfield Regeneration**
p. 118–19: Image by Y3C Studio (Zhu Yufan Studio), used with permission.
p. 121–22: Images by Zheng Xiaodi, used with permission.
p. 124: "Waterfront park in Xuhui District, Shanghai" by Shengyuan Zheng, used with permission.

**Toward a Space of Capability**
Chinese to English translation by Chendi Zhang.
p. 126–27: Image by Baihui Zhuo, used with permission.
p. 129: "The Quarry Garden in Shanghai Chenshan Botanic Garden" by Y3C Studio (Zhu Yufan Studio), used with permission.
p. 130: "Shougang Industrial Park, Beijing" by Y3C Studio (Zhu Yufan Studio), used with permission.

**City Beautiful**
English to Chinese translation by Shengyuan Zheng.
p. 134: "Shanghai skyline" by Shengyuan Zheng, used with permission.
p. 137–40: Images by University of Pennsylvania Weitzman School of Design Jing-Jin-Ji megaregion studio, courtesy of Marilyn Taylor, used with permission

**Considering China's Future Public Realm**
p. 142–43: "Playing basketball at waterfront park, Xuhui District, Shanghai" by Shengyuan Zheng, used with permission.
p. 145: "Jing'an Temple Park, Shanghai" by Shengyuan Zheng, used with permission.
p. 147: "Tianzi Lane, Shanghai" by Shengyuan Zheng, used with permission.
p. 148: "Street chess in Shanghai" by Shengyuan Zheng, used with permission.

**Park City**
p. 152–53: "People's Park, Shanghai" by Shengyuan Zheng, used with permission.
p. 155: "Park, Shanghai" by Shengyuan Zheng, used with permission.
p. 156: "Sitting on West Lake in Hangzhou, Zhejiang Province" by Shengyuan Zheng, used with permission.

**The Garden Laboratory**
p. 158–59 : "The Garden Laboratory" by Li Cangshuan, courtesy of Liu Hui, used with permission.

p. 161: "Groundcover plant community in different seasons" by Liu Hui & Li Cangshuan, used with permission.
p. 162: "Groundcover plant community composition model" by Liu Hui & Li Cangshuan, used with permission.

**Participatory Construction of Public Urban Landscapes**
p. 166–73: Images courtesy of Liu Yuelai, used with permission.

**Landscape: From Aesthetic Experience to Public Health**
p. 174–75: "Pedestrian overpass in Shanghai" by Shengyuan Zheng, used with permission.

**Healing Landscape and Beautiful China**
p. 180–81: "Running trail at waterfront park in Xuhui District, Shanghai" by Shengyuan Zheng, used with permission.

**Market, or Museum?**
Chinese to English translation by Yifan Cai.
p. 186–90: Images by Jason Zhisen Ho, used with permission.

**Between Sapience and Sentience: Four Remarks in Response to Beautiful China**
p. 196–97: "Aerial view of Pingjiang Historical Blocks, Suzhou" by Shengyuan Zheng, used with permission.
p. 200–01: *The Autumn in Que and Hua Mountains* by Zhao Mengfu, public domain.
p. 204: "Richuan Village, Yongjia" by Shengyuan Zheng, used with permission.

**Credits**
p. 214–15: Image by Shengyuan Zheng, used with permission.

p. 200–01:《鹊华秋实图》, 作者赵孟頫, 公共版权。
p. 204: 永嘉县日川村, 郑盛远拍摄供图, 已获得作者许可。

**特别鸣谢**
p. 214–15: 郑盛远拍摄供图, 已获得作者许可。